OUT OF THE BLUE
ALETA'S STORIES

ANGELA BOWEN

PROFILE PRODUCTIONS
www.jenniferabod.com

Out of The Blue: Aleta's Stories by Angela Bowen

Book Design: Khari Klein

Cover Designs: Virginia Blaisdell

Back Cover Photo: Nick Venden © 2011

Photo Enhancement: Virginia Blaisdell and Alan Shwachman

Photo Selections and Research: Jennifer Abod

"Turning Point 1989" by Jennifer Abod

"Cornelia's Mother" was first published in *Sing, Whisper, Shout, Pray!: Feminist Visions for a Just World*

ISBN-13: 978-0615720333
ISBN-10: 0615720331

Profile Productions
www.jenniferabod.com

Photographs and Selected Writings

Front Cover: Irene Shwachman © 1960
With the permission of Alan Shwachman

Irene Shwachman's photos are part of the Freedom House Collection, Archives and Special Collections Department, Northeastern University. Shwachman's complete photographic collection resides at The Center of Creative Photography, Tucson, AZ.

Two Little Girls: Unknown Photographer © 1948
Archives and Special Collections Department, Snell Library Northeastern University, Boston

Girl on Bike: Irene Shwachman ©1962

Bus Stop: Irene Shwachman ©1962

Cambridge view of Boston: Jennifer Abod © circa 1983

Nubian Woman: Reverend Brenda Haywood © 1970. Cover image appeared on "Conditions Five," the first widely distributed collection of Black feminist writing in the U.S.

"Out of the Blue" lyrics by Jason Will and Nemo Henry © 1947

"Apologies to all the People in Lebanon" by June Jordan from Directed by Desire. The Collected Poems of June Jordan © 2005. With permission of June Jordan Literary Estate trust; www.junejordan.com

DEDICATION

To all the Aletas in the world
and to all who nourish and cherish them.

PREFACE

Dear Reader,

Aleta's Stories are based in both fact and fiction. I grew up in Roxbury in the 1940s and 50s, and vividly remember the different neighborhoods where my family lived. These characters represent a combination of people I have known, although some are pure fiction.

Growing up, I considered my life boring until I discovered dancing; as an adult, I came to appreciate those growing up years, despite how poor we were. My household was rich in conversations, political perspectives, life lessons, and culture, which I enjoyed weaving into the stories.

I have lived with *Aleta's Stories* for a long time, and over the years I have shared them with friends and family. The comment that delights me the most is that they remind people of their own lives. I hope this is true for you.

Angela Bowen

Out of the Blue: Aleta's Stories

This poignant collection is about a journey of self-discovery, childhood innocence and experience. Aleta's stories offer a rare window into the thoughts and actions of a little girl growing up in Boston's inner city in the 1940s and 50s. Her stories are unflinching, unpredictable, timeless and universal.

Table of Contents

Roxbury 1940s

Cornelia's Mother

Cornelia's mother got headaches. And whenever she had one, she'd lay on the couch in the living room with the shades pulled down, a wet washcloth over her forehead. Aleta thought it was so romantic, just like white women in the movies who had fainting spells. Well, she guessed that made sense, too, since Cornelia looked more white than black.

Aleta met Cornelia in the schoolyard at the beginning of their third grade school year. She was new there and Aleta had noticed her for the past couple of days standing by the end of the fence, just back from where the girls jumped rope at recess.

"Hi, you want to play jump rope?" Aleta asked.

"No, thanks," Cornelia said. She shook her head quickly, but smiled a bit, showing a tiny dimple on her left cheek, just below where other people had dimples.

"You don't like to jump?" Aleta asked.

"I'd rather just watch. I'm not very good at it."

"Well, neither am I. I just do it anyway."

"Oh, come on, I've been watching long enough to know better. You're just trying to make me feel good."

"Did it work?" she nodded. They laughed.

They were quiet, examining one another. Cornelia's eyes took in Aleta's dark brown complexion, broad nose and full lips; her nappy hair with braids so tight they curled up at the ends, her ashy face and skinny legs, scuffed shoes and tumbledown socks. Aleta wondered if the sash of her dress was torn. She played so roughly that the sash, tied in a bow in back, would often tear out from the seam at one side of the waist and hang down with the bow still tied, without her even noticing. Just as often, the hem would tear as she climbed over a fence and jumped to the ground.

Aleta noticed first that Cornelia was exactly her height—they were both short for their age—but that's the closest she came to looking like Aleta. Cornelia was the color of coffee ice cream, and just as smooth. Her hair, just a shade darker than straw, was parted in the middle and pulled straight back from a high, round forehead above inquisitive light brown eyes only a little darker than her hair. Two perfect thick braids reached barely below her shoulders, with a rust-colored bow sitting precisely above the end of each one.

"What grade are you in?" Aleta asked.

"Third."

"I thought so. Well, how do you like Miss Bellamy?"

"How'd you know I have Miss Bellamy?"

"That's for me to know and you to find out," Aleta teased, stepping back into the game to take her turn at the rope.

The next day at recess Aleta spied Cornelia beside the fence and, ignoring the jump rope crowd, moved over to join her. Cornelia's large brown eyes watched her steadily as she approached. For a fleeting moment Aleta wished she didn't have to wear glasses—she actually liked them, but she'd heard people say she had such pretty eyes, it was a shame she had to wear them. For the first time, Aleta agreed. As she came closer, Cornelia's smile spread and the dimple appeared.

"I know how you knew I have Miss Bellamy," she announced.

Aleta grinned, "Yeah, how?"

"Because there's only two third grades in the school, and you're in the other one."

"Give the girl a gold star," Aleta said, standing tall and sweeping her arm toward her. They fell out laughing because Miss Bellamy was famous for giving out those little gold stars.

"Have you gotten any of them on your papers yet?" Aleta asked. Cornelia nodded, still smiling.

"Oh, the girl is smart, too." Aleta said.

"What do you mean, *too?*" Cornelia asked softly. Aleta suddenly became tongue-tied. What she'd *meant* was that she was smart as well as pretty, but of course she couldn't say it— nobody talked that way in their neighborhood.

"So, where do you live?" Aleta asked instead.

That afternoon Aleta walked Cornelia to her house slowly to make it last, before they ran the next two blocks home.

Cornelia was fun to be with. She and Aleta would march along three-legged, arms around waists, their middle legs so perfectly matched that they could gradually increase to a very fast run, then slow it down whenever they decided, without even saying a word or exchanging a glance. They made up word games with clues and codes that no one else knew the rules to—the kind you can play with only one person, because if you tried to include other people, the magic would disappear.

One of their favorites was called *fast.* Aleta would start with a word like "sidewalk." Cornelia would have to say a word beginning with the second letter, so she'd say "igloo"; then Aleta would say "door," Cornelia would say "end"; and so on. But the rule was, you had to say each word faster than the one before, so sometimes they'd be saying words that didn't even make sense, shouting them faster and louder until they just fell out laughing.

The only trouble they had was with Cornelia's mother. She was sick a lot because she was so worried about Cornelia's father, who was overseas fighting "in the service," a phrase Aleta had gradually come to realize was entirely different from the way Mama used *in service*, as in, "Cousin Mary lives *in service* at the Kaplan's out in Newton and only comes into town on Thursdays." A color photograph of Cornelia's father sat in a gold frame on the table at the side of the couch, only inches from where the mother's feet rested when she was lying down with a headache. With her head propped on pillows, Cornelia's mother could look directly into her husband's face. He wore a brown soldier uniform with three gold stripes on his sleeve. A visor-cap sat on top of hair that was the same light shade of gold-brown as Cornelia's. His eyes were darker than hers, but not by much, and he looked directly out at you with a serious but kind expression. His complexion too was a little darker than Cornelia's. Cornelia's mother was paler than the both of them, and except for her skin color and her smooth black hair and eyes, she could have been his sister.

She liked Cornelia to stay in the house, unlike the rest of the kids Aleta usually played with who could wander freely around the neighborhood. Cornelia and her mother lived in a five-room apartment on the second floor of a three-decker red brick building right across the street from a park. Five rooms, for just one woman and a small child! Aleta's family had seven rooms for a big family of eight. Cornelia's home was sunny, quiet, spacious and extremely neat—an apartment where dishes never piled up in the sink. Aleta had never seen a roach there, but she just knew that if one showed up, Cornelia's mother would catch her breath, in that little quiet "Ooh" kind of in-taking gasp.

They were the kind of family who had *dinner* instead of supper, who ate meals all matched up with vegetables and potatoes and meat, and never ran out of food or had to have cereal for supper. They wore housecoats and slippers and had pajamas and nightgowns, not old shirts to wear to bed. And of course, Cornelia would *never* wet the bed. In Aleta's house, besides wetting the bed, they also left clothes lying around and had to run from one room to another looking for their coats when it was time to go out. Sometimes they'd have to rob the bulb from one room to light another, leaving the first room in total darkness while they took care of whichever matter was more pressing elsewhere. They ran out of toilet paper and had to shout from behind the closed bathroom door for someone to bring a piece of crumpled-up newspaper . . . or *something!*

The closed bathroom door also signified Aleta's only moments of privacy. In a family of seven children, with various sets of friends constantly coming and going, sitting and gabbing, eating, smoking, playing cards, arguing, listening to music and dancing, among other things, it took a bit of scheming just to find a quiet corner to read. Aleta's solution was to lock the door and sit on the laundry bag in the corner. But her solitude never lasted longer than 10 minutes, and the last five of that was usually accompanied by impatient banging on the door and loud shouting. It seemed as if no one ever thought about going to the bathroom until *she* got in there. She'd keep reading while part of her mind measured the level of intensity in the voice outside the door, relinquishing her concentration and slamming the book shut only when the timbre of the voice matched the urgency of the message, "COME OUT OF THERE RIGHT NOW, RIGHT NOW, WILL YOU *PLEEEEEZE*?"

Aleta couldn't imagine Cornelia having to put up with such confusion. But then again, she didn't have to put up with anything near what Cornelia did if she wanted someone to come visit.

"Can you come play at my house tomorrow?" Cornelia asked.

"Sure I can. Right after school?"

"Wait, first I have to ask my mother, and then I'll let you know."

"Well, why didn't you ask her first?"

"I don't know. It makes me nervous to ask, so just in case you couldn't come."

"Why shouldn't I be able to come? You know I can come whenever I want to. It's just to play, it's not like staying over or something."

"Don't get mad, Aleta. My mother's not like yours. You know that."

"I'm not mad. Only dogs get mad."

Cornelia was silent. Then she said, "Okay, then, you're not mad, you're angry."

"Well, why does she have to make such a big commotion about everything, anyway?"

"How do I know? Do you think I like it?" Cornelia's face was starting to turn red. She was the only colored person Aleta had ever seen turn red when she got upset.

"Okay, okay," Aleta said, "You can let me know what she says tomorrow. Just calm down, we don't want you to get apoplexy, do we?" Aleta just discovered the word, and looked for occasions to use it. Cornelia smiled. Even though Aleta sometimes lost patience with Cornelia's mother, part of her was fascinated by the way they lived. So neat. So orderly. The mother so carefully taking care of herself, lying back among the pillows on the couch.

Aleta and Cornelia would play dolls or jacks quietly in Cornelia's room or on the back porch—which had linoleum on the floor—and, if they laughed out loud, Cornelia's mother would say in a whiny voice

Aleta had never heard from an adult, "Cornelia, please, dear, I have a headache."

"Sorry, Mother," Cornelia would say. Aleta had only heard white kids in the movies say "Mother," instead of "Ma" or "Mama" or Momma." If they let the porch door slam, it would be, "Cornelia, if you can't be quiet, your friend will have to go home. Mother is feeling ill." **Ill!** Nowhere outside of a book had Aleta ever heard that word spoken aloud except by teachers who used it instead of "sick" when they sent you to the school nurse.

"All right, Mother, we'll be quiet," Cornelia would say, looking pleadingly at Aleta, who tried not to show what she was thinking, but sometimes it was beyond her control, and she'd feel her eyes roll, totally on their own.

Aleta never knew who else played with Cornelia, but she knew they'd have to have plenty of patience, which she believed she had. Besides, Aleta did a lot of free, unsupervised kind of playing with other friends and with her brother Ralphie—roaming the city as they liked, sneaking on buses, playing jump rope and dodge ball, climbing fences, stealing empty milk bottles from the crates in back of the corner store and reselling them to the proprietor. Cornelia didn't have Aleta's carefree type of life, so she could be generous.

But one thing she found it hard to be generous about was that Cornelia's mother never offered her anything to eat. It seemed as if they just didn't think about food. And since Aleta and Cornelia hardly ever went outside to play, there was no way to swipe any goodies from the grocery or the drugstore—a form of fun Aleta always had with anyone else she hung out with. Still, even if they had been able to go outside, something just told Aleta she couldn't even suggest such a thing to Cornelia.

One other thing: Aleta was a smart kid. She lived across the street from the library and spent a lot of time there. Aleta's library card was her most prized possession. On Saturdays, when her brothers and sisters and most of the other kids in the neighborhood went to the movies, she went to the library. They were allowed to take out only two books at a time, so Aleta would go early, pick up two books, rush home and read them, then double back before the library closed at 5:00pm, and pick up two more to get her through until Sunday.

Aleta had also been class-spelling champ every year since first grade. But Cornelia's mother assumed that she could spell over Aleta's head, as she did to Cornelia, who sometimes pretended not to understand, just so she could get to hear more.

Cornelia's mother's sister looked enough like her to be her twin and, whenever she visited, they were always smirking at each other while they spelled words about Aleta being "nice" for coming from such a family" and how it was good "training" for Cornelia to "share" her toys with Aleta since she'd probably "never" have an "opportunity" to play with such high "quality" things otherwise. Aleta never let on that she could decipher such "complicated" words. They almost made Aleta laugh, trying so hard to spell over her head that they were sometimes misspelling! But what made Aleta the angriest was for them to think she couldn't even spell simple four-letter words.

One sunny afternoon, Cornelia's mother called the girls in from the back porch where they were cutting out doll clothes. They came into the kitchen, where Cornelia's mother and aunt sat listening to Stella Dallas on the radio and drinking tea from pearly china teacups that matched the pot. Aleta's mother had a set just like it in her dining room. The outsides were a delicate yellowish grey color, while the insides were a faint pink with rainbow colors swirling through. A line of gold ran around the rim of the cups and around the teapot, about two inches above the base. The tea set at Aleta's house sat behind the dusty glass doors of the china closet and only came out on rare occasions, like when Mama's women friends came for a club meeting, or on Thanksgiving when the kids were allowed to drink carefully out of them. Mama said the set had been a wedding present. Somehow it seemed right that Cornelia's mother and aunt would use theirs on a daily basis, just like it seemed right for Aleta's family not to.

Cornelia's mother asked them to run an errand. "Would you and Aleta run down to the corner store for me? I need a few things for dinner."

The aunt chimed in, "Yes, this is a perfect time to go while you have an extra pair of hands. Your mother doesn't feel well, and while I'm here I might as well prepare a good meal for the two of you." She was older than Cornelia's mother by four years and seemed to like to show it.

The thing was, going to the store for Cornelia's mother; she didn't know the rules of the neighborhood. If you asked a child who wasn't yours to go to the store, you told them to spend a penny on candy—two cents if you didn't know them well or if they seldom did errands for you. If it was a child visiting, you simply gave them a snack or, if you didn't have anything suitable in the house, you asked them to bring back something you had included in your grocery list—cookies or an apple, maybe—then you presented it to them. Having had experience with Cornelia's mother, Aleta knew better than to expect anything out of this trip. She would simply go along as a favor to her friend.

"Here, Cornelia," said the aunt, handing Cornelia a piece of paper. "Write this down." As she dictated the grocery list, Aleta stood silently watching Cornelia write in her careful script. They did penmanship every day in school for 20 minutes—the Palmer method, the teacher said—and Aleta envied Cornelia's handwriting. Suddenly, the aunt said, "You take so long to form your letters. Here, give me the paper." She reached out and pulled it toward her, then snatched the pencil from Cornelia's fingers.

Watching her friend's face fall, Aleta said in a snappy voice, "Are we in a hurry or something?" The aunt's hand paused as she turned her whole upper body sideways in her chair to look at Aleta. Her eyes traveled slowly from Aleta's face, to her feet, and back up again. Then, looking Aleta squarely in the eyes, she said, carefully spacing each word, "Well, *some* people like to have their dinner at a *particular* time every day, not just *haphazardly* whenever it happens. So, yes, we *would* like to get these groceries back here rather soon, if it's all right with *you*."

Cornelia took the list and went down the stairs. When they got outside, Aleta said, "Whew, what a witch you've got for an aunt." She wanted to say something about Cornelia's mother, too, but you didn't talk about a person's mother unless you absolutely couldn't help it—and only if the kids said it about their own mother first. Then you could agree with them, but only a teeny little bit. Cornelia said about her aunt, "Oh, she's all right most of the time. And she really likes you. She always says you're so smart, I should stick with you and I could learn something." Aleta couldn't answer that with anything nice, so she just changed the subject.

When they got back to Cornelia's building, Aleta opened the door to the upstairs hall and turned to hold it open for Cornelia. She was struggling with the bag, so Aleta said, "Here, I'll take it." Fair was fair, and, since they had forgotten to tell the man to pack the groceries into two bags, Cornelia had carried it all the way from the corner and up the outside steps. So Aleta took it upstairs.

As the girls entered the apartment, Cornelia's mother smiled slyly at her sister "Look, now Cornelia's got an M-A-I-D." Behind her, Aleta heard Cornelia catch her breath. They stood in silence. The clock above the table ticked loudly, each second pushing time ever so slowly along. On either side of the clock, screened windows showed the light green of new spring leaves moving gently in the breeze. Yellow curtains with tiny raised brown dots drifted playfully up and down at the windows. As Aleta turned to her friend, her eyes devoured in one glance the peaceful quiet of the kitchen with its polished red and brown tiled floor, spotless white sink and matching stove, where a shiny kettle emitted steam in a comforting, steady stream.

At the brown, enamel-topped table with a red rim running around the edge, Aleta saw the two sisters sitting catty-cornered, staring at them from wide, dark eyes.

As Aleta handed her friend the bag, she choked out, "Bye, Cornelia." For one moment, Aleta looked into Cornelia's loving brown eyes filled with tears, and wanted to reach out to hug her, but she could hear the sisters begin to snicker together behind them. Aleta turned to the door. Her hands were so sweaty; she couldn't grip the knob to turn it. She knew Cornelia was willing her to look back at her, but Aleta just couldn't raise her eyes. She could feel them all looking at her belt hanging off her dress, her drooping hem, her tumbledown unmatched socks and run over shoes. Besides, her nappy hair needed rebraiding and her lips were too big. Tears were swelling up at the back of her throat and her eyes were starting to burn.

Aleta's hand slipped round and round the knob until finally, with one mighty yank, she flung the door open and stumbled slowly down the stairs, gripping the rail to keep from falling as the hot tears rushed from her eyes. Aleta heard Cornelia's mother calling after her, "Aleta...Aleta? Don't you want to stay and play with Cornelia?" Then, to her sister, in an uncertain voice, "Do you think maybe she understood us?"

"Of course not," announced Cornelia's aunt in that know-it-all tone. Then she said, "Cornelia, did you understand what your mother just spelled?"

Aleta never heard her answer. She never went back. Cornelia and Aleta never played together again.

Aunt Frannie and Blanche

Aleta laughed out loud as she watched Ralphie drag the heavy fur coat out of their apartment to the hallway and push it over the railing. Then he leaned over the stairwell and screamed, "Here, don't forget your hump-backed buffalo!" Aunt Frannie's deep tremolo drifted back up to them, "Don't you dare handle my coat that way, you *pissy-smelling little* . . ." she yelled at Ralphie. "See, Barbara, you see what he did? Animals! Wild animals you're raising here!"

"Don't you worry about my children," Mama shouted down the three flights of stairs. "You go on home and raise your little lords and ladies. These animals won't trouble you if you just stay away from the zoo!" and, grabbing Aleta and Ralphie by their arms, she yanked them inside, slamming the door so hard it shuddered in its frame, then bounced back open. They dashed across to the living room window, pushing aside six-year-old KayKay, who stood in the middle of the room staring in disbelief at Mama whom she'd never heard yell at Aunt Frannie or at any other grown-up. Aleta and Ralphie peered out of the window, trying to see their aunt, who would have to pass under their third floor window on her way home. Ralphie was trying to push up the window when Mama, standing in the doorway, spoke in a trembly voice, low in her throat, "Just leave it."

"You know you're not supposed to open that window, Ralphie," KayKay said in her specialized-for-tattling, singsong manner, glancing over at Mama for approval.

"Oh, shut up," Ralphie muttered, reaching back to pinch her arm.

"Ouch! Mama, Ralphie said shut up. And he's pinching me."

"Be quiet, KayKay, just be quiet," Mama said in a low, choked-up voice as she turned from the doorway and marched off down the hallway toward the rear of the apartment. KayKay looked at her retreating back, stiff with rejection of them all, and her face began to break up. Anticipating KayKay's wail, Lilly said quietly from her corner of the couch, "Come here, KayKay. I'm going to sing you a song."

Aleta and Ralphie, with a quick eye signal, slid as one, out of the living room and down the hall. KayKay looked longingly after them but could not resist snuggling up to Lilly for the song. She wasn't going to let this moment escape, since Lilly usually ignored her.

Ralphie and Aleta sat on the floor in the corner of the bedroom next to the radiator. With the closet door pulled open, they were hidden from anyone passing by and glancing in from the hallway.

Ralphie was chuckling about the look on Aunt Frannie's face when Mama told her to *get out*.

"She's been asking for it for a long time, don't you think?" he chortled.

"Yeah, I guess she went too far this time," Aleta agreed.

"So, what happened? Ralphie asked. "I just came out of the room in time to see Aunt Frannie come flying up the hall with Mama rushing behind, yelling about people who want to "out-American the Americans.""

"Well," Aleta began, "I was still kind of asleep when I heard her knock."

Early that Saturday morning, Aunt Frannie had come knocking on the door. Mama said she liked to come early on purpose to catch them and the house in a more tumbled up state than it always was anyway, so she could have more to complain about. Lilly, four years older than eight-year old Aleta was reading, so she answered the door right away and led Aunt Frannie into the living room. Aleta stepped through the doorway just in time to see Lilly's eyes darting around to find the least offensive place for their aunt to sit.

In a corner of the armchair, two dolls lay sprawled together, one with an eye missing and two patches of hair torn from her rubber head, which was twisted backwards. The other had an arm and a leg missing from opposite sides of her body. A dirty piece of blanket was flung next to them. Dominoes lay in a heap in front of the same chair. Half-dozen comic books, their pages worn from a thousand turnings, were strewn across a couch with cushions so worn that grayish-white stuffing was beginning to peek through the once red upholstery of the cover. At one end sat a checkerboard, a dozen checkers scattered meagerly on top. A corner of peanut butter sandwich curled dismally on top of a section of newspaper, folded carefully and waiting patiently on the soiled arm of the couch.

The girls glanced at one another, seeing the room in a way they did only when their aunt came to visit. Their heads turned simultaneously toward Aunt Frannie as she slowly and disdainfully surveyed the room, her eyes finally coming to rest on Aleta in the ragged, dingy, long shirt she wore to bed. "Oh, uh, hi, Aunt Frannie," Aleta said, trying to hide one ashy leg behind the other.

"You know how she just nods her head and blinks those big round eyes at you real slow, right, Ralphie?"

"Yeah, yeah, sure," Ralphie said. "So go ahead. How'd Mama get into the fight with her?"

"Well, just wait a minute; I'm trying to tell you."

Aunt Frannie was big and tall like Mama, but where Mama was slim, Aunt Frannie was large and solidly fleshy. Her head jutted forward a bit, and the merest suggestion of a round mound sat just below her neck in back. Aleta hadn't really noticed it before Ralphie started calling her *the buffalo*. She was very dark, with a smooth clear complexion of the kind Mama called rosy. Her skin glowed. In response to Aleta's greeting, she nodded slowly, her nose and lip turned up just enough so that if you didn't know better, you might think she was smiling.

As their aunt lifted her head for another glance around the room, Mama came up the hall and, taking in the situation right away, said, "Oh, Frannie, come on back to the dining room. I'm having a cup of tea with my friend Blanche." Aunt Frannie pulled her fur coat tightly around her, as if afraid it might touch one of the walls, and followed Mama down the long hallway to the dining room. Lilly and Aleta glanced in relief at one another.

Lilly drifted down the hallway into the bedroom she and Aleta shared with KayKay and Ralphie and, picking up her book, headed back to the living room. Aleta rushed into the bedroom, where Ralphie was scrunched down under the covers, his slender ten-year-old body barely making a mound on the bed. She paused only long enough to pull on her clothes so she could slip down the hall and hear what was going on. Lilly would never do that. Once she decided that she didn't like someone, she never went near them if she could help it. She said that being around people she didn't like *got on her nerves*. Aleta didn't have *any* nerves.

She got to the dining room just as Mama was saying that Blanche was about to have a second cup of tea, and would Frannie like one. Aunt Frannie nodded. Mama reached into the glass cabinet to get out one of the pearly pinkish gray teacups that matched the teapot. As she started to the kitchen to wash the cup and saucer, Aleta stepped through the dining room door, hand outstretched. "Want me to wash it, Mama?"

Mama's eyes twinkled as she said, "Alright, just be careful. Move the other dishes out of the sink first." Aunt Frannie's sniff was audible.

There was never a dish left in the sink of her painfully neat apartment. They offered you a glass of lemonade and before you even finished swallowing, they took the glass out of your hand and washed it while you were sitting right there. Another thing: there wasn't a book to be found on the premises. That was something Aleta could never get to the bottom of. Where did they keep their reading material? She had never seen any of her six cousins, the two boys and four girls, between ages sixteen and twenty-four, reading.

As Aleta carefully carried the cup and saucer into the kitchen, she could hear Mama saying that although she had known Blanche for only a few months, they had become very good friends. Blanche added, "Yes, I tell my friends that sure, Barbara Skerritt's skin may be black, but her heart is white as snow.'"

Aleta ran the water gently, listening intently. Somehow she knew that Mama wouldn't tell Aunt Frannie how she had met Blanche. Rinsing the cup and saucer and placing them upside down on the drain board, Aleta went into the dining room to get the teapot, asking, "Should I fix the tea, Mama?" Mama slowly nodded her eyes grateful.

Aleta took the pot into the kitchen. As she scooped out the wet tea leaves, she heard Aunt Frannie's deep voice, "So, how do you know Barbara?"

Blanche laughed. "We kind of met over the clothesline. Wouldn't you say that, Barbara?" Mama nodded silently, trying to give Blanche a signal not to say any more.

"Why a signal?" Ralphie asked Aleta. "How did they meet anyway? I never did know."

"Well, it was all about my dress," Aleta said. "You know that brown and green plaid dress with the white band around the bottom and around the edge of the sleeves?"

"Come on, Aleta, I don't pay any attention to your clothes. Just say what happened."

"O.K., O.K., hold your horses. Gee!"

Like most people in the neighborhood, Mama usually hung their clothes on the back porch. But when there was a really large wash, people hauled their laundry to the communal plot two blocks away because it had about twelve long lines and was wide open to the sun, so clothes dried faster. Frannie had almost that many lines to herself in her own back yard because she and Uncle Horace owned their own house. The neighborhood understanding was to send someone from your household periodically to check, and as soon as your clothes were dry, you took them down.

Mama had sent Lilly first that day to check on the wash. Then Aleta went and returned with the O.K. and then she and Mama took the wagon and went to bring the wash home. When there was one empty space on the line, Mama wondered aloud what had been in that space, but right away Aleta knew that her favorite dress was missing.

"I cried all the way home," she told Ralphie "and every time I thought about it for the next week, I felt sad. Then, one day I saw my dress on this little white girl in school. You could tell it wasn't hers. It was far too big. I whispered to my friend Ellen that it was my dress, and Ellen said that 'of course it was', she'd seen it on me enough to know it anywhere. I'm not sure that's true because I only wore it to school once or twice, but you know how Ellen loves a good fight." Ralphie nodded impatiently. "She was telling me to go over to this girl and get her told. But I just walked up to her and said, 'Say, where'd you get that dress?' I could see she knew something was wrong by the way she looked down and wouldn't answer, but she was so little and scraggly, I wouldn't bother her. But I told Mama about it. The next day, I walked behind her when she went home. I stayed way back and didn't bother her, like Mama told me, but I saw where she lived. So the next Saturday when Mama was off, we went to her house, and that's how we met Blanche."

"I understand your daughter has a dress that belongs to us," Mama said as soon as Blanche opened the door.

"I don't have anything of yours," Blanche said, standing in the doorway, hand on her hip.

Mama described the dress, and then asked, "Where did you get it?" Blanche didn't answer. Mama said, "Want to know where I last saw it?"

"Listen, I found it," Blanche said. "It was on the ground by the fence. I didn't know it belonged to anyone."

"We just want it back, that's all," Mama said, one foot planted firmly just inside the door.

"Look, I'll give it back. Just let me have a couple of days to wash it, and then you can have it."

"All right, then," Mama said. She was silent a moment, looking around the poor little apartment. After a while she said, "You know, a very nice Italian woman I work for has girls a little older than mine, and she gives me clothes for them. She gave me that dress. Sometimes I could . . . well, if you want, I'd be glad to share them with you."
Blanche smiled so wide, you could see where two teeth were missing at the side of her mouth. "You're a good woman, you sure are. Would you come in for a cup of tea?"

"And that's how Blanche Mahoney and Mama became friends," Aleta told Ralphie.

"Hey, that's a good story. So, O.K., now what happened this morning with Aunt Frannie?"

"Well, when I brought the tea back into the dining room, Blanche was getting up to leave and she said, 'I'd better get home and make some dinner for my boys and my daughter. It was nice meeting you.' Aunt Frannie just blinked her eyes and said nothing.

"I guess she got the hint, huh? Ralphie said. "The air was mighty chilly, and she didn't want to get frostbite." They chuckled.

"Yeah. So Mama walked Blanche up the hall and said good-bye. When Mama got back, Aunt Frannie started bragging about how good her boys were doing in their studies and the girls in their music lessons, and their beautiful clothes, and how she didn't have to work because her husband worked hard every day and wanted her to stay home and take care of these children so they would have some discipline. Then she got going on Mama about her good-for-nothing sons hanging around the street, and all the usual stuff. Finally, she really got going on Lilly, which I pretty much expected to happen.

"That Lilly sees me in the street and barely opens her mouth to speak." said Aunt Frannie. "She's a mighty rude little thing. It's bad enough to raise young men to be so trifling, but at least they have manners. When they see me they always act respectful. But that willful one."

"You know she was born feet first, Frannie. I'm sorry, but I can't do anything with her. She just has her own ways. I tell all my children to respect you as my older sister."

"Well, if that's so, you need to call her in here right now and make her apologize."

"No, she'd just be worse the next time. She might even insult you to your face in front of people," Mama said.

"Ralphie, I swear Mama enjoyed saying that to her."

"It's true, though, we know Lilly. She can come up with some good ones, can't she?"

"Yeah," said Aleta. "Probably stores them up from all those movies she sees."

"Okay, go ahead."

"Well, then Aunt Frannie started on the house and how it's always a mess, and that Mama should keep us out of the living room. Actually, she called it the *parlor*—that way she'd have some place *decent* for visitors to sit." Mama said, 'This is their house. A home is for people to enjoy, not for show.'"

"And Auntie said, 'Well, you certainly couldn't *show* this one anywhere.'"

"Then Mama said, 'I struggle by myself to make a home for these children. I don't ask you or anybody else for anything. I'm not killing myself to make this rent every month just to keep them holed up in their room so visitors can be comfortable, whatever few times they come. If people don't like how my house looks, they shouldn't come.' Then Aunt Frannie said, 'I suppose you mean *me*? I'm sure the way you keep your house is all right with Blanche and people like her, but it's not what I'm used to. Anyway, I wouldn't have someone like her around my children.' Mama just stared at her."

'No? What's wrong with her?'

'You're always with the books and all the high talk about you're raising them to be educated for something *better*. So she's the something *better* you want them growing up around?'

"Mama said softly, 'Not to be *around somebody better*, but raising them *for something better*. Never mind. You wouldn't know what I'm talking about. But Blanche? She's a good woman, a widow struggling to make it just like I am.' 'Hmmph. A grass widow, more likely.'"

Ralphie interrupted, "What's a grass widow?"

"I'm not sure, but we can ask Lilly."

"O.K., never mind. Just go ahead."

"So then Mama said, 'Frannie, people could be saying the same thing about me. Anyway, it doesn't matter. Just leave Blanche alone. Grass widow or not, she's raising her children alone too. Besides that little lonely girl, she has two boys, one Ralphie's age and one older like my big boys; and she's one of the finest friends I've ever had.'

'Oh, yes, a fine friend. *Trash*, nothing but low white trash. Hmmph. Gaps in her mouth where teeth should be. You'll have anyone at all around these children. No wonder they're growing up so wild.'"

"Mama jumped to her feet so fast, Ralphie, the chair fell over behind her. 'My children are not wild. They respect people who respect them. Their father and I raised them that way on purpose, not to be slaves and doormats. And Blanche is *not* trash. Being poor and white doesn't make her trash. She's more woman than you'll ever be because if anything happened to me, she and my other friends would fight to keep my children together, but you wouldn't give a damn!'

'I'm your big sister, Barbara. Watch how you talk to me.'

'Some sister! When I was seventeen and left Montserrat and came to this country, our mother told me that you'd look out for me. What did you do? Charged me nearly my whole week's wages for a room in your house that I only saw for one day of the week because I lived "in service." Put me out of your house because I dated an American man instead of a West Indian. You never respected him as my husband, the way I did Horace, but then, Horace was West Indian, not some overeducated American Negro, as you called him, with more books than bread to give his children, who didn't act like a father—talking and laughing and playing with them instead of disciplining them with a good strap. Didn't you say that? Then when he died, you told me if I didn't put my children in an orphanage, I'd never receive help from you because by the time I finished raising seven children I'd only be fit for the grave. Well, you keep your fancy house; keep your fancy fur coats and your put-on fancy way of talking. I'll take Blanche any day. If there's any trash around this house, it's you. Now, *get out!* Aleta, get me the broom, I'm sweeping *trash* out of here today!'"

"I came running from the kitchen with the broom," Aleta continued. "Aunt Frannie jumped to her feet, snatched her fur coat from the chair, and scurried out of the room. Mama chased her up the hall sweeping at her ankles. Aunt Frannie was shouting, '*Don't touch me with that broom. No! No!* You know it's bad luck. Stop!' She was skipping and dodging up the hall, picking up her feet as best she could. Her coat dropped and she hopped over it and kept going."

"Mama was right behind her. 'Bad luck? Oh don't worry, Frannie, it's only backward, superstitious folks who think that, remember? Isn't that what they told you in that high Episcopal Church you switched to because all the *best* class of West Indian go there? Don't worry about a little broom. You don't believe in all this country voodoo nonsense, remember? Hypocrite! Trying to out-American the Americans!'"

"By then Aunt Frannie was tripping all over herself getting down the stairs, and you came out of the bedroom and grabbed up her coat and threw it after her."

Ralphie was rolling around pounding the floor with his fist, his lithe body shaking with laughter; every time he tried to catch his breath, he snorted.

"So you think," he said between gasps, "we're finally rid of her?"

"For a while, at least, maybe even for a whole year. But you know Mama. That's still her sister. So don't think we're rid of Aunt Frannie for the rest of our lives, or anything like that."

"Well, a year would help, right?" asked Ralphie.

"Yeah, a year would be *juuust beautiful.*" Aleta sighed.

KayKay stepped into the room, and, peering at them around the opened closet door, asked, "Why is a year just beautiful?"

Ralphie pushed the closet door shut so he could lean closer to KayKay. He beckoned her with his finger and she leaned her head in against his. He whispered solemnly in her ear, "Because in a year you'll be seven, and that's the magic year that *tattling* stops." KayKay stood still for a moment, then turned to the door and rushed out of the room.

Aleta and Ralphie waited for a few beats, and then mimed in perfect unison along with KayKay's voice drifting back to them down the hall, "*Maaama, Ralphie called me a taaattle-tale.*"

Baked Beans and the Big Man

Although Mama wasn't adept at wielding the old, worn out strap that her husband used to sharpen his razor, she kept it around as an on going threat, signaling what she *might have to do* if any of her children drove her to use it. Granted, she couldn't generally deliver more than a few half-hearted licks (along with tons of preaching), but she managed to bear down with something approaching determination whenever Aleta lied to her and sneaked over to Cousin Velma's. It was the one place Aleta could remember Mama ever forbidding her to visit—which might have been why Aleta developed such a fascination for going there.

Whenever Velma visited, she enticed eight-year-old Aleta to her apartment with whispered promises of trips downtown to the movies, money she had waiting for her, dinner out at restaurants, or new toys. Although Velma's promises never materialized—and after the first few times Aleta knew they never would—she returned repeatedly because of the tantalizing tingle of dread she felt when she was around Velma. Aleta sensed Velma's bad intentions even though she didn't quite understand why what she suggested was wrong.

Cousin Velma was around twenty. She was tall, slim, light on her feet, and very dark, with a cute/ugly pushed-together face, and sly, watchful eyes set deep into prominent eye-sockets. One day Aleta went to Velma's apartment with a promise of sweets. But instead, when she arrived, Velma teased Aleta into bed with her and a big, stalwart man with satiny black skin and a deep, happy laugh that made her join in, even though she didn't know what they were laughing about. Velma kissed and tickled him, poked and slapped at him until his "thing" stood up as high and huge around as his forearm.

When the Big Man saw Aleta staring in silent awe, he grabbed the sheet and draped it over himself. Giggling, Velma pulled the sheet off him and flung it to the floor.

"Ooh, look, it's so tall," she said, pulling down his "thing" and letting it go so that it bounced back up. "Boing," she shouted.

"Aw, Velma, come on, Aleta doesn't need to be looking at all this. Get her clothes on and get her out of here. I'll pay for a cab to send her home."

"Okay, I'll send her home—after I come back. I'm just running down to the corner to get some more beer. I'll be right back."

"No, Velma, no, I bet you won't be back for hours. Come on, take the kid out of here with you; then get beer if you want. This isn't right, you know."

"Oh, stop worrying, you big, sweet baby." Velma leaned over and kissed him inside his ear, a loud, wet sound. "If you want to stay and play with me," she said, her voice growing cold, "then just wait till I get back with the beer. Aleta's okay, aren't you, honey?"

Without waiting for an answer or looking directly at her, Velma reached down to the floor and grabbed her skirt, then came to her feet in one motion, wrapping and tying the waistband as she slipped her feet into her loafers. She stepped away from the bed, ran a comb through her hair, and then moved quickly to the bedroom doorway, snatching her jacket from the back of a chair on the way.

Inside Aleta's head a voice was screaming, *No, I'm not okay, I'm scared! Please, Velma, don't leave me, please.* But Aleta said nothing, watching longingly as Velma stood in the doorway, one hand high on the doorjamb, one fist pushed into her waist, one slim ankle crossed over the other, the sole of her loafer perched firmly on its tip. Velma's eyes danced from one to the other as she said with a slow grin, "Well, have a good time, you two. And don't do anything I wouldn't do." She turned quickly, pulled the door closed firmly, and hummed her way down the stairs.

They laid there in silence. Aleta kept her eyes pinned on the door, refusing to turn her head toward the Big Man. His husky, deep voice, which had been ringing with laughter earlier as he and Velma sipped beer and chased each other around the bed, throwing Aleta back and forth between them, was now a soft, sad whisper.

"You scared?" Aleta couldn't answer. "Don't worry; I'm not going to hurt you." Aleta kept watching the door. The Big Man said gently to Aleta, "Hey, come here."

He pulled her close, holding her against his barrel chest for a couple of interminable minutes. Aleta could feel his heart racing— or was it hers? Then the man kissed Aleta on top of her head, sat her up and said, "Go put your clothes on."

Aleta stumbled to her feet and grabbed her clothes from the chair where Velma's jacket had hung, and made her shaky way across the tiny hallway to the bathroom. Glancing in the mirror over the sink just before she closed the door, Aleta caught the reflection of his broad, naked back as he sat up on the other side of the bed, looking down at his feet on the flowered linoleum floor.

The Big Man walked Aleta home in the chilly fall air, holding her hand all the way. Aleta had never held such a huge hand before, never felt like such a protected little girl. This must be how it felt to walk down the street with a daddy; just like her brother Wesley and the other older kids had done before Aleta's father died.

When Aleta and the Big Man reached Aleta's building, he asked, "Your mother home?" "Yes," Aleta said, adding quickly, "but you don't have to come up." He said firmly, "That's okay, I want to." They climbed to the third floor still holding hands, although it was awkward to keep holding on as they came around the turns on the stairs. It was Mama's only day home—Saturday, her baking day. The aroma of beans and molasses met them aggressively on the stairs. Aleta pushed open the door that was standing slightly ajar, and she and the man stepped through just as Mama came walking up the hall. Mama stood stock still, her eyes taking them in with one swift glance. Raising her eyes from their locked hands, to the Big Man, she said quietly, "Hello. Do I know you?"

"No, ma'am, my name is Willie Brownlee. I met Aleta at your niece Velma's." They exchanged a long look.

Finally, letting out a deep breath, Mama said, "Would you like to have something to eat? I'm just about to get the beans out of the oven."

Willie let go of Aleta's hand and rubbed both of his together, his lips spreading into a broad but watchful smile. "Thank you, I'd appreciate that."

Mama sent Aleta to wash her hands and get out the plates, and to stay in the kitchen until they came to join her. As they moved down the hallway, Aleta heard each of Mama's footsteps striking hard on the bare wooden floor and felt her eyes boring into her back.

A few minutes later, when Mama and Willie entered the kitchen, Aleta knew everything was back on track. She bustled the dark brown crock of beans out of the oven and took off the cover. The steam rose, wrapping them in the warm, savory aroma of beans, molasses, onions, pepper and salt pork. Then, reaching up to the built-in warming shelf at the back of the black stove, Aleta removed the steamed Friend's brown bread filled with plump raisins that she'd heated up right inside the can. She pushed the cylinder of moist bread through from one open end of the can to the other, and it slid smoothly onto the plate. She began slicing. Willie sat across from Aleta, wriggling in anticipation as Mama dished their bowls of piping hot beans and laid round slices of brown bread on a plate between them.

"Where's the other kids?" Aleta asked, mouth full.

"At the movies," said Mama, her eyes seeming to say, *and if you would just go with them on Saturdays you'd be better off.* But Aleta could tell she was happy and satisfied to have her sitting safe and cozy in the warm kitchen with her, eating. The only sound was the low hum of the electric clock over the sink and the juicy-mouthed chewing of bread and beans.

When Willie got up to go, he leaned across the table and said to Aleta, "You going to remember what I said to you when we were walking home?" "Yes, I'll remember," she said quickly, not wanting him to say anything more in front of Mama. Then he turned to Mama and thanked her about six times for the meal.

"You make me feel good, you know? And not just for the meal. Aleta's lucky to have a Mama like you."

Mama reached up and patted his shoulder. "Thank you, Willie. And you're a good man too. Bye, now. You be careful." Aleta was waiting to hear whether either of them would say he'd be coming back to visit. But Mama didn't offer, and he didn't either. They both seemed to know why not—although Aleta didn't. But, after escaping a licking with the strap (which Aleta knew she deserved, and was almost welcoming), and seeing that Mama was feeling so happy that nothing bad had happened to her, she wasn't going to spoil things by asking any questions.

They stood side by side at the window, watching Willie's broad body moving away from them up Townsend Street. Aleta was wondering if Mama was sorry too, that he couldn't be their friend.

Then she said, "What did he tell you when he was walking you home?" Aleta didn't answer, knowing Mama would say, *I told you the same thing, didn't I?*

"Did he tell you to stay away from Velma?" Aleta nodded. "What else did he say?"

"He said not to ever trust Velma because all she's interested in is dragging everybody down, and he said she's an evil person."

Mama nodded briefly, a small, whispered, "Yes, yes," escaping her lips. Then she looked up the street again, where Willie was now a tiny figure hurrying in the distance. Mama shook her head slowly and said, "But he can't get back there *fast* enough. *Just look at him go!*"

Aleta turned and walked away. She didn't *want* to look at him go.

Hail Mary

Mary Pauline and Mary Theresa, or simply Pauli and Tess, were the most fun of any of the girls who arrived at camp for the second session the summer Aleta was nine. They were beautiful, short, sturdy white girls with tawny skin, short brown tousled hair and merry brown eyes that actually sparkled when they laughed, which they did constantly, showing square shiny white teeth. They were both eight, which the rest of them had the hardest time understanding because they were sisters, but not twins. They kept explaining that they were born 10 months apart, and that soon Pauli would be nine while Tess remained eight for a good long time; but it was all too complicated for any of them to grasp.

In any family Aleta had ever known, one's sister or brother was always the next year in age or more. When Aleta said something about it to Mama, who was the camp cook and spent the summer in a cabin pretty close to Aleta's, she hmmphed and shifted and Aleta figured that there was something not quite right in being only ten months apart, but Mama never explained why.

Pauli and Tess were popular with everyone, including the counselors, but for some reason they decided to allow only Aleta into their private world. Some kids were fun because they were good at athletic pursuits or because they knew how to talk about stories they read, or they could invent new games. None of these reasons applied to the sisters. What was special about them was that they were the first girls who ever told Aleta Catholic secrets, which she had always wanted to know. Being around nuns had always scared Aleta. She could never look directly at them. But about Catholicism itself Aleta was very curious. Pauli and Tess had lots of mysterious knowledge to impart, like what constituted a sin, the different kinds of sins; about rosary beads and the confession box and Holy Communion and novenas and holy water and the Stations of the Cross; and about purgatory (which is what happened to babies who weren't christened), and all that sort of business. Aleta was fascinated by how much there was to know; how sure of the information they were; and how many different prayers they had all memorized.

They sneaked their beds close together, which was against the rules. Then they'd hold hands and listen to "Taps" and let big tears gather in their eyes and roll down their cheeks because the bugle music was so sad and beautiful and Pauli said it was played for all the soldiers who died in the war. Then, whispering in the dark, they'd tell Aleta all sorts of stories and never ask her anything—which was smart of them, as far as Aleta was concerned, because compared to theirs, her life seemed pretty boring.

Pauli and Tess already had nine children in their family, with only two older than them, and their mother was having another baby soon after they got home. They knew a lot about taking care of babies. They told Aleta about the nuns in school, the mean ones and the nice ones; about the priest who drank too much and liked to feel up their eleven-year-old brother; about the boy their age who lived downstairs from them with webbed fingers and who still suckled his mother's breast. And, they taught Aleta *The Hail Mary*.

"No, stop showing off, you're speeding so fast she'll never get it," Paulie said.

"O.K.," Tess slowly intoned "Hail Mary, full of grace, the Lord is with thee, blessed art thou among women, and blessed is the fruit of thy womb, Jesus. All right, Aleta, now you say it." And together they all began. Finally, Aleta got it right three times in a row.

"Holy Mary, mother of God, pray for us sinners now and at the hour of our death, amen. Go ahead," Pauli urged. They chanted along with Aleta until she could say it in rhythm with them. Then they had to say them both together, first The Hail Mary, then The Holy Mary.

"*Now do the hokey pokey while you say it,*" whispered Pauli.

"How can you do the hokey pokey in bed? You have to be standing up to dance!" Aleta said. They laughed so hard they had to crush the pillows over their heads.

"No, you know, down here with your finger." Oh, this sounded like Aleta's friend Marie back home.

"Come on, you know how, don't you?"

"No," Aleta admitted.

"Don't you ever play with yourself and tickle until it makes you *sneeze?*" asked Tess.

"No, I never did."

"O.K., you keep rubbing and tickling and pressing in there until it feels so good you want to yell or laugh, but you can't because you're not supposed to be doing it, so you act like you're sneezing," Tess whispered, more softly than usual, cupping her hand around Aleta's ear.

Then Pauli said, "Gee, Aleta, you're pretty old not to know this stuff; you're even older than me."

Aleta was feeling pretty dumb, which Pauli could always manage to make her feel, so she said, "Well, why aren't you supposed to do it?"

"Because it's a sin, silly," said Tess.

"Then won't you go to hell?"

"No, you go to *confession*; remember? I told you about confession!"

"Oh, yeah, I remember now." Aleta felt even dumber than before.

"So, come on, you want to learn, don't you?" asked Tess.

"Yeah, I guess so."

"Here." Pauli stuck her finger under Aleta's nose. "Smell." Aleta took a sniff.

"Like it?"

Aleta was too embarrassed to say so, but she didn't like it at all. It smelled like dirty underpants.

"Here, smell mine." Tess stuck her finger under Aleta's nose. Aleta didn't breathe.

"You didn't sniff, I can tell," Tess whispered, much too loud.

"Girls, no talking out there, you're going to get the A side punished," yelled counselor Gwen. Aleta and the sisters' cabin, The Robins, was divided in two, A and B, with cots on each side and a counselor's enclosed room in the middle containing two beds. Now they had to be really quiet because immediately following Gwen's pronouncement, indignant "shushes" had come from five other cots on their side of the cabin. Now the three girls sensed listening ears in the dark.

They lay motionless for about 10 minutes, which felt like an eternity. Just as Aleta was drifting away, a hot breath penetrated her ear. Tess was whispering, "Come on now, let's go," and they began chanting softly, "Hail Mary, full of grace," while their fingers rubbed between their legs and they murmured and rocked, sometimes grunting, sometimes saying to each other or themselves, "Mmm, good Mary, mmm blessed fruit, mmm, Sweet Jesus, mmm, it feels so good, doesn't it, Aleta?"

Aleta would say, "Yeah, it sure does, mmm." But really, she was just waiting until they finally got to the sneeze so they'd be done.

Nearly every night for 10 days they'd tell Aleta stories, and then she'd pretend she was hokey pokeying too. But she never quite got the knack of it. Aleta finally decided that they had been so busy teaching her the Hail Mary they'd never gotten around to telling her exactly where she was supposed to be touching. And, Aleta was never interested enough to *press the issue*.

Sometimes, less often lately, when Aleta hears a stray Hail Mary or even that quick exclamation some old—usually women—Catholics still make, "Holy Mary, Mother of God," she gets a faint flash of those two beautiful little girls writhing and twisting their hips while they chanted and giggled and murmured and made themselves *sneeze*.

Marie

Nine-year-old Aleta raced down the stairs from her third floor apartment, shoving her arms into her coat. She reached the first floor and pulled open the inner door to the hallway just in time to hear the outer street door slam and see her brother Ralphie through the glass door as he jumped the six cement steps to the sidewalk and dashed up the street. A rush of cold air flowed in, reminding her of forgotten hat and gloves. For a fleeting moment she considered going back upstairs, but knew that if she did, she'd miss walking to school with Ralphie and their around-the-corner neighbor, Gus, who was in Ralphie's 5th grade class. The boys had sneaked off on some brief adventure last night right after supper, and she figured this might be her only chance to find out what they'd been up to. She'd better hurry.

Aleta jumped the three steps in the marble hallway, yanked open the street door and rushed down the steps to the pavement, just in time to catch a glimpse of her friend Marie coming around the corner from her right. Aleta muttered to herself, "Oh, please, not today, Marie." Aleta turned her head left and yelled quickly, "Ralphie, Ralphie, wait!" Ralphie and Gus were punching each other on the arm and laughing, Ralphie's head thrown back, his blue and brown hat bright in the biting cold. Aleta could hear Ralphie's high cackle that always made her smile even when the joke was on her. Gus's brown quilted jacket was wide open, both sides flying behind as he walked against the wind. He dodged Ralphie's blow, spinning around and coming to an abrupt halt so her brother would miss. Gus was grinning so wide she could almost feel his buckteeth hurting from the cold. How'd they get two blocks away so quickly?

Aleta and Ralphie used to walk to school together every day. He was always ready to leave the house first, but he'd wait for Aleta, only slightly impatient. Aleta did everything slower than Ralphie, including dressing and eating. Lately, though, he'd begun dashing out of the house as soon as he was ready. Aleta always seemed to be chasing after him these days. Now she stood on the sidewalk calling Ralphie as he sped away. In the split second it took for her voice to reach him in the distance, she had the feeling that he would hear her but refuse to answer. Aleta took a step in the boys' direction just as Marie came to a stop beside her. Then she saw Ralphie turn to her and yell, "Well, come on, then, hurry up."

At the same moment, Marie spoke from her right side, "Aleta, wait, can I walk with you?" Aleta groaned inside. If she waited for Marie, she could forget about catching up with the boys. Although they might wait for Aleta, they didn't like walking with Marie. They called her Missy Prissy; in fact, most of the kids in the neighborhood called her that. Marie never ran, but walked in even steps, like the little lady her grandmother had taught her to be.

She wore a green wool coat with a black velvet collar. A brown and green plaid scarf was tucked around her neck and tied under her little pointed chin. Her narrow dark face with large round eyes looked out from under the bonnet of a green hat that matched her coat.

One of Marie's green-gloved hands gripped the double handles of a brown leather book bag that matched her shiny brown shoes. She was the only kid in the school who carried a book bag. She said she didn't care if the other kids thought it was funny—it used to be her mother's music bag, and Marie loved it. She shined it with shoe polish, just like she did her shoes, three nights a week.

Aleta could hear Ralphie and Gus both yelling at her now. "Are you coming or not, Aleta? Will you make up your mind?" She looked up the street. They were shifting from foot to foot, hands jammed deep in their pockets. She turned back to Marie, who was waiting quietly for her decision. Suddenly Marie flashed a sad little smile, "It's

O.K. if you do." as if to say, she could understand why Aleta wanted to go with them.

Aleta shouted toward the boys, "Go ahead. I'll see you at school."

"Oh, great! Thanks for making us wait," came Gus's smart aleck voice, the words spouting from his mouth on little billows of cold white smoke. Ralphie nudged him to let it go. They started off again, running. Marie watched Aleta pull her coat together, running her hands down from the collar, searching for buttons. The solitary top button hung by two threads, but Aleta felt a large safety pin sitting in a strategic second button position. She remembered that she had pinned her coat together with it yesterday morning, meaning to find a button when she got home from school and ask her sister Lilly to help her sew it on. Actually, it had been more like three days ago, come to think of it. Aleta wanted to use the pin now to hold her coat together where it mattered, but she wouldn't let herself to do it with Marie looking on, so she pushed her hands into her pockets and pulled her coat close together. If Marie said even one word about it, she'd run off and leave her walking alone.

"Come on, let's go," Aleta said. As soon as they started walking, Marie began talking. The other kids around their way thought Marie was quiet, but Aleta knew better. Marie didn't play or talk much with anyone else, but sometimes when they were alone together, Aleta could hardly get a word in.

Now Marie was saying, "I would've helped you pin up your coat, but my fingers are all bruised. I don't even know how I'll hold the pencil in school today." Aleta sighed inside as she asked, "Why, what's the matter with your fingers?"

"You know," Marie said softly, looking off up the street.

"Were you doing that again?"

Marie nodded.

"I thought you said you were going to stop," Aleta said. "Why do you keep doing it when you know what happens?"

"I don't know. I don't mean to, but I can't help it. It makes me feel good."

"But is it worth it when she's always catching you?"

"Mostly it is, but it was so bad, *so bad* last night."

Marie's grandmother was a short, fat woman with smooth black skin; a high, fake little light voice that sounded as if it belonged in a much younger and slimmer woman; a small head sitting on top of a neck that looked like separate large ropes of coiled sausage resting on one another; little beady eyes that looked straight inside you; and the lyingest smile that a grownup ever aimed at a child. She was doing her best to raise Marie into a *decent-God-fearing-woman* because Marie's mother was off in New York somewhere, *doing-God-only-knows-what*, which is what The Grandmother said every time she mentioned her.

Aleta didn't visit Marie often because Marie had so much housework to do and also had to practice the piano for an hour every day. Her grandmother always said, "practice makes perfect." Her lips would pull back into a satisfied little smile, as if she were saying something new.

Whenever Marie was allowed to have Aleta visit, the girls would look at the pictures of Marie's mother that sat on top of the piano in the living room, on the buffet in the dining room, and hung on the walls in the hallway. She was beautiful. She looked something like Marie, and nothing like The Grandmother. But where Marie had a tiny, neat little face with a pointed chin, her mother's face was heart-shaped with big brown eyes and full lips that always seemed to be smiling. Marie's smile looked like her mother's, but Aleta saw it emerge only when she and Marie were alone. Where The Grandmother's eyes were flat and black and mean like a snake's, the mother's were warm, round and loving; and where The Grandmother and Marie had very dark, smooth skin, the mother's was more a merry brown chocolate color. Aleta could just imagine the music tumbling out of her with joy, instead of in the careful, obedient way Marie made music. Marie played the notes correctly, but it never quite sounded like music.

The pictures of Marie's mother showed her every which way imaginable: as a baby sitting on a bed with a white ruffled blanket spread around her; three years old in a pink dress, sitting on a high piano stool, her back to the piano, her feet crossed at the ankles and dangling in the air above the floor, hands in her lap; at age five in blue ruffles, bowing on a stage beside a piano; around eight-years old, receiving a prize onstage in a long yellow gown; about ten-years old, sitting on a pony, while dressed in leggings and a brown woolen jacket. And there were so many more. The photos began in babyhood and continued to about age sixteen, when suddenly they stopped.

Marie's mother (according to Marie's grandmother), was heading toward a career as a concert pianist because *she had talent* and had practiced *faithfully* for an hour every day until she was 8, then for 2 hours every day until she was twelve, then for 3 hours a day— 2 of those days with a special tutor *very, very expensive*. So much money had been put into her musical career *before she messed up her life*.

Marie's mother had run away with a boy. That's how she had Marie. When she was in the hospital in New York, she was very sick, and the boy who was Marie's father had disappeared, so the doctors had sent for Marie's grandmother, who went and brought Marie and her mother back to Boston. When Marie's mother got better and wanted to leave, Marie's grandmother kept the baby. She said that Marie's mother wasn't fit to raise a baby, so she'd just better go on about her business. The Grandmother gave one little satisfied nod whenever she said that.

"But she's going to send for me when I'm ten," Marie had said just last week, looking straight at her grandmother.

"Well, I know where you get such fool ideas," said the light little voice, "but you just better be happy you've got Granny to keep you away from that no good. No telling how you'd end up. You're too much like her already, if you ask me." The little head bobbed again. Once.

Marie quickly interjected while The Grandmother was taking a breath, "Granny, can Aleta come into my room and play dolls with me?"

The Grandmother's head swiveled quickly toward Marie, then turned toward Aleta, the flat eyes boring into her while she pursed her tiny mouth into a sour little bow.

"Yes, go on, then; just keep that door open. No telling *what* you all want to really be doing in there."

Aleta had no idea what she meant, but the words made her feel nasty somehow, so she tried not to look at The Grandmother. Mama always told her to turn her back on mean and ugly people, not to let them take up her attention. But, try as hard as she could to ignore The

Grandmother, Aleta felt those evil eyes boring into her back as she followed Marie to her room.

Aleta always had the feeling that she and Marie and The Grandmother were playing some kind of game. If The Grandmother won, Aleta would be forced to stop playing with Marie, who would then be left with nobody to talk to. Aleta would win if she could ignore the meanness and try to imitate Marie's Missy Prissy ways in The Grandmother's presence (although Aleta never thought for a second that she was fooling The Grandmother). And Marie would win if she could keep acting the part of Missy Prissy until her mother came and got her or until she grew up and got out of that evil house. Since The Grandmother didn't know or care anything about who Marie really was, Marie could have some fun along the way if she acted out her part and was *very* careful.

Although most of the neighborhood kids didn't know it, Marie was really fun. She was smart and could mock anybody, from kids in the neighborhood, to teachers, and even her grandmother. And, she could make up really good stories. When, occasionally, she was allowed out to play, the girls worked out schemes for Marie to sneak over to Aleta's house for brief periods, where she could see how real families lived, and could even hear kids argue back with their own mother sometimes. At first, Marie had found that hard to believe. But, once she'd heard Aleta and her mother have a discussion that allowed Aleta to come out on top and get her way without her mother being angry, Marie changed her mind. Marie kept bringing it up for a long time afterwards, and was incredulous when Aleta told her that it was Mama who had taught them that the only way they could make people understand what they wanted was to argue for their position without anger.

One time Marie and Aleta decided to work on The Grandmother to let Aleta stay overnight. Aleta didn't really want to stay over, but after Marie had pestered her for weeks, she'd given in and asked Mama.

"Marie wants me to stay overnight, Mama. Can I?"

"Why?" Mama asked.

"Just because she gets lonesome with no other kids in the house."

"What does Mrs. Taylor say?"

It took Aleta a few seconds to remember that that was The Grandmother's name. She always talked and thought about her as "Marie's grandmother," or, to herself, as "The Grandmother."

"We don't know yet."

"Oh, I see," Mama said. "You're trying it out on me first, eh?"

"Yeah, Mama, she's just so mean; there's no reason for Marie to ask her if you're not going to let me go anyway."

"Well, I don't know. If the woman doesn't want you there, why go? I don't send my children anywhere they're not wanted."

"It's for Marie's sake. I don't really like being there. Her grandmother—well, it's not just me, her grandmother wouldn't want anybody there. And nobody else would go anyway. Who else could she even ask?"

"Doesn't she have any other friends?" Mama was looking at her intently. Aleta shook her head.

"So, why you?"

Aleta shrugged. Mama said softly, "You know, your little sister KayKay doesn't have any friends either. Why doesn't that bother you?" "Come on, Mama," Aleta responded, eyes down, shifting her feet, "just tell me if I can go. I won't argue any more if you say no."

Mama was silent. Aleta couldn't resist one more, "Please, Mama?"

A big sigh came out of Mama. "Alright, then, but I don't want any foolishness out of that woman, you hear me? You have a home, and if she doesn't treat you right, you come back here right away, you hear me?"

"Yes, I hear you. Don't forget, she hasn't said yes yet. But if she insults me I'll come home. I promise."

Mama didn't know the half of it. Aleta met The Grandmother who delighted in insults. If it wasn't Aleta's clothes, it was her hair, or she was so skinny she must not get enough to eat. Or where was her father? Had her mother been married at all? Aleta had long ago decided to ignore The Grandmother's attempts to push her away from Marie.

Finally, Marie gained her grandmother's reluctant permission, and the girls chose Friday for their overnight stay. That evening, after The Grandmother had come into the room three or four times with warnings to stop talking, staring intently down on them each time,

Marie had fallen asleep. But Aleta, lying awake in confusion, had seen The Grandmother's shadow cast on the wall several times in the night, whenever she opened the door from the kitchen to peek in at them. The next morning, Aleta had left right after a quick breakfast of cold cereal. She never stayed overnight again, nor had Marie ever asked her; and they'd never discussed that night.

But now, as they pushed their way to school against the wind, Marie began telling Aleta what was so especially bad about the night before that had made her hide her hands in her coat pockets.

"Well, last night Granny told me that after my piano practice, she wanted me to do my reading for school and then go right to bed because she had to go out to a meeting at church, and she didn't want me staying up without her being home. So I was at the piano when she called goodbye. I heard the back door slam. I did everything just like I was supposed to. Just *exactly* like she told me and in the same order. Then I went to bed."

"I was lying there thinking about Mommy and wondering if we'd ever be together. Before I even knew it, I had my hand on my chest and the other one was down between my legs. I was kind of rocking and humming and I was almost asleep, when I heard a big loud crash, right up close, like the ceiling was falling in on me. I was so scared, Aleta, my heart almost jumped out of my chest. You know that closet next to my bed, the one that just stands by itself, like a great big cupboard, but it's not built into the wall?" Aleta nodded.

"Well, the door of the closet swung wide open and smashed back against the wall and Granny was standing there with the leather strap, her eyes big and shiny. She was waiting in there the whole time, all the whole evening."

As Marie told the story, in gasps and bursts, Aleta felt like she was in the dark room with Marie, her heart in her mouth, eyes stretched in fear as the hulk exploded in fury. No escape!

"Didn't I tell you to keep your hands off yourself, you nasty little whore? No, no don't take your hands away now. I caught you, you lying little *bitch;* just keep 'em right there. That's right, just keep on rubbing, you like it so much. Pull up that nightgown higher, get it up there. I'm going to break those fingers, tear up that slit for you, make it so numb you ain't ever going to feel good down there again!"

The strap kept whacking Marie's fingers as they rubbed her little nubs of breast. 'Keep rubbing, hurry up, faster, rub faster you little nasty whore, you're just like your mother, faster, open up your legs wider, lemme in there, I got to get it, beat it, bust it, oh, rub, rub, oh, hurry up, faster, you know you love it, love it, oh, rub it, love it, get it good, oh, oh . . ."

The strap whistled through the air and cracked, tearing flesh as her voice grew louder until she was screaming gibberish in high pitch, her arm rising higher and descending harder as she whacked chest, hands and shoulders, moving down Marie's belly to beat on the fingers working frantically between her legs. She finally tumbled onto the sobbing child screaming, "Oh, Jesus, oh, my sweet Jesus, oh, God."

"I thought she died on top of me," Marie said "but then I could hear her breathing fast, and loud, and spit was drooling down the side of her mouth, and her clothes were all wet, and she stunk so bad I thought she peed on herself."

"Oh, Marie, how awful!" Aleta croaked past the dryness in her throat, "How—how long did she stay there?"

"I don't know, I was just trying to keep my head still so I could breathe. The top of her body was lying across me, but I could breathe if I just didn't move. After a long time, she got up and went out of the room."

"Oh, Marie, poor Marie! And what about this morning? How did she act? Did she say anything?"

"She acted the same as always, but she didn't look right at me.
Fixed my oatmeal, and gave me my castor oil and the half of orange like she always does, and told me not to talk in class. But when she gave me my nickel, she looked at my hands and said, 'You know I had to beat you last night for Jesus. He don't like you doing things like that, I been telling you. You know God don't like ugly, so you be a good girl today for God.' Aleta, do you think she's right? What do you suppose God thinks about what I do to myself?"

"I don't know, Marie. I guess we're both too young to know. But, I can tell you what my mother says about God and Jesus."

"What? Tell me."

"She says that Jesus was a good man who loved people, especially little children, and that grownups who like to frighten children about

God are always the people who are doing some very bad things themselves. My mother thinks those are the most evil people there are. I'll bet she means people like your grandmother."

"Really, Aleta, she said that?"

"Yeah, well, I don't remember the exact words, but something pretty much like that." In her head, Aleta said, "Sorry, Mama, but I guess it's close enough to the things you would say, and I needed help to get Marie through this. We can discuss this later."

"Thanks, Aleta," Marie said. You know, I feel better already."

"Good, then can you walk a little faster? I'm freezing."

Marie laughed. "Sure. And, Aleta . . ."

"I know, I know. Don't tell a soul what you told me. Don't worry."

As they entered the schoolyard, the girls separated to hurry to their respective lines and wait for the bell to ring.

"Marie," Aleta called.

"Yes?" Marie paused, looking over her shoulder.

"Come here. Put your bag down for a minute."

Marie put the bag down next to her feet. Aleta reached out her hands and Marie placed hers in them. Slowly, Aleta pulled off the green gloves. Both girls looked silently at the swollen hands, stripped and bruised and turning colors, and the skin broken in some places, already closed over in others. Such tiny little hands, Aleta thought.

"Listen, tell her if she ever does that again, you won't be able to play the piano for a long time. Then don't play the piano for at least a week. Tell her it hurts too bad."

"Oh, I don't know if I could tell her that, Aleta. I'd be too scared."

"Well, tell her that if the piano teacher sees them, she might want to know what happened, and you think she'd better not come give you your lesson this week. I don't think she'd want anybody to know about this."

"But I like my teacher to come. It's the only time my grandmother acts nice to me."

"Marie, you have to help yourself. Sit at the piano and act like you're trying, but that it hurts too badly. And it probably will. Let's think about this. The biggest thing she wants is for you to play the piano. First your mother, then you, right? So if she hurts you, you can't play the piano, right? Simple."

"But I want to play the piano too. Not just for her. I like it." "Well, if you're going to get anywhere with your grandmother, you can't let her know that. You have to act like you're doing her the favor of your life by playing at all. Come on, girl, don't you get it?"

"How do you know it'll work?"

"I don't *know* it will, but when we have problems, my sister and my brother and me, we think about how to do something to take care of it. And we try it. Then if it doesn't work, we try something else. We hid our mother's strap one time, and she never found it."

"You really did?"

"Yeah. The only one we didn't tell was my little sister KayKay because she tells everything. But I can even show you where it's buried."

"What did she do when she found out it was missing?"

"I think she knew we hid it, but after she asked about it a few times, she didn't bother about it. She didn't really know how to use it all that well, to tell you the truth. My Mama's not much of a hitter."

"Maybe she could take lessons from my grandmother."

The girls' laughter was shaky.

"Granny would be a great teacher for that, I bet. "Still," continued Marie, "it must be easier to do things like that when there's more of you. I can't do anything by myself. I'm too scared of her."

"Yeah, it's good if there's more of you, that's true. My brother Ralphie and me, we come up with the best ideas. But, you, being alone, just about the only thing you *can* do is refuse to play the piano. But, see, you can't show that you're refusing. Come on, Marie, you have to try, O.K.?"

"I don't know. I'll think about it."

"Here, let's put your gloves back on." Aleta pulled Marie's gloves on carefully, then bent down and picked up her book bag, handing it into the right hand, which Marie held out.

Aleta was acutely aware that this more bruised hand must have been the one Marie had had between her legs, the one The Grandmother had threatened to beat right off her arm.

"What are you going to do about this hand, Marie? It's going to take a long time to heal."

"Oh, I guess I'll just have to learn how to use the other one for a while. *Practice makes perfect, you know,*" she said in the exact voice of her grandmother. Aleta raised her eyes and saw the little smile turning up the corners of Marie's mouth. Her head bobbed once like her grandmother's. Her eyes smiled warmly into Aleta's, like her mother's.

"You mean you're going to keep on . . .?" Aleta laughed out loud and Marie joined in, then reached up to whisper in Aleta's ear,
"Because it feels good."

They realized at the same moment that several lines of kids were looking at them curiously. "Listen, Marie," Aleta said quickly as the bell began to ring, "meet me at the corner after school. Let's walk home together."

"O.K, if you say so."

"You, me and Ellen and all the other kids too, O.K.?"

Marie's smile disappeared. "Are you sure?"

"Yeah, I'm sure." Aleta flashed a grin. "Don't worry; I'll take care of it. Now, how about you? You sure?"

Marie nodded quickly and whispered, "O.K." Then she tucked her book bag under her arm and stepped into line, lifting her little pointed chin.

Marvin

"Marvin, Marvin, come on, sweetheart, drink your milk. Please, Marvin, just a sip for Momsky," went the refrain as she rounded the corner and headed toward Aleta in her monotonous shuffle. Marvin's mother held a silver cup, milk swaying over the rim and falling in droplets onto the sidewalk in front of her. An especially large slosh rose in an arc and poured in a little fountain onto her pink plush slipper as she came to an abrupt halt in front of Aleta. Her eyes roamed Aleta's face for a moment, and finally met hers in recognition.

"Oh, did you see my boy Marvin, uh, hello, hello, uh, uh . . ."

"Aleta," she said with a jab of annoyance. Aleta didn't feel like telling Marvin's mother that he had just gone lumbering by, grinning delightedly at the head start he had on her.

"Yes, right, uh, Aleta yes," she muttered, projecting her head forward to peer at Aleta intently, concentrating on her name, but puzzled by Aleta's attitude. Aleta was pretty puzzled by it herself. Usually when Marvin and his mother started into their crazy game, she watched them, as amused by the spectacle as the rest of the neighborhood.

Mrs. Koppelman was an unkempt woman of indeterminate age, with frizzy gray and brown hair that Aleta had seen combed neatly only once in all the years her family had been living across the street from them; that was on the afternoon that Marvin and Aleta were honored as the top boy and girl spellers in the third grade. Aleta could never understand why there couldn't be just one best speller. The girls were better, anybody could tell that, because it took about 2 or sometimes even 3 weeks to eliminate all but one of the girls, and the boys were always done in 2 or 3 afternoons. If there was only one winner, Aleta would have had first place to herself for the past two years. But, both Marvin and Aleta had received the medal with the red and blue ribbon and the trip downtown to the *Globe* newspaper office with all the winners from the other schools. If there was only one winner, the five dollars would have been all hers, instead of having to be split two ways. Even more important, Aleta's name would have been all by itself on the right hand side of the blackboard with her grade next to it: Aleta Skerritt, grade 3. The sixth grade winners' names came first, the boys then the girls; after that came the fifth grade winners, then the fourth. And there they stayed all through the rest of the year, in every classroom in the school. When the blackboard was washed or, once a month, inked, the teachers wrote the names in again. They hadn't had the Spelling Bee yet in Aleta's fifth grade year, but for the first time there was a chance that Aleta might lose, so she was secretly making up lists and studying on her own. Thelma Kosciusko, her only rival for the girls' top spot, was new to the school that year. Aleta wouldn't have been surprised if Thelma was off by herself somewhere doing the same thing, hiding the grievous sin of caring enough to want to win. That's the way you had to be around their neighborhood. After the first few years of winning, Aleta knew a lot of kids would have been happy if she lost, so she insulted them further by acting as if she paid it no mind. Aleta's teachers didn't pass out spelling lists or encourage them to study for it. They just sprung it on them with no notice. Aleta guessed that spelling was supposed to come naturally or not at all.

Anyway, standing there, on the sidewalk just around the corner from her apartment building facing Mrs. Koppelman in her usual housecoat and slippers, Aleta could see that with the half a block head start he'd had, Marvin was going to win this round. The thing was, Aleta realized just recently that she didn't care to see the scene played out in its entirety any more. As Mrs. Koppelman stepped around her, and crossed the street heading back to her apartment building, the familiar litany began again, "Marvin, Sweetheart, Momsky needs you to drink just a little . . .   Marvin. . ."

Mother and son were locked in a ridiculous battle. When the four rooms of their second floor apartment became too confining for their struggle, Marvin would burst out of the house and run around and around the block with gleeful, thick-bodied awkwardness as she trailed behind, causing the watching neighbors to place bets on how it would end this time. The most usual outcome was for Marvin to stumble and fall flat. We'd never seen anyone fall in such an inert, unmuscled way, and we used to wonder how anyone who fell like that would ever dare to run again. Whenever Marvin fell, his mother was able to catch up with him and kneel down on the concrete sidewalk, pulling his head up just enough to force the last few drops of milk past his unresisting lips.

The second way it could end was for Mrs. Koppelman to simply give up. Despondent and muttering, she'd shuffle back into the house with an empty, or near-empty, cup. Once Marvin realized she was no longer chasing him, he would wander back into the house, or stay outside until she threw open the window to call him in. Another outcome of their game was for Marvin to gain so much ground in his race around the block that he'd come up close behind Mrs. Koppelman and, just as she passed the stoop, he'd slip into the house, pounding loudly up the stairs and locking the door after him; whereupon, she would backtrack to their building, ascend the stairs and bang the cup on the door, begging him not to be such a bad boy to his poor Mumsky, because she wasn't feeling well, and anyway, he'd be sick if he didn't drink his milk. If Marvin persisted in keeping her out, Mrs. Koppelman would summon one of the kids playing outside, prevailing upon one of them to go across the street to Sid's Market, her husband's grocery store, and ask him for the key so she could get in.

It seemed as if Aleta had always known the Koppelmans — at least the mother and son. She'd been living in the neighborhood for six years, and they were already there when The Skerritt family moved in. But it took several years for Aleta to connect Marvin, her bright but lazy classmate and pudgy outcast neighbor, with Sid the grocer. Aleta's apartment building was on the corner of Humboldt Avenue and Townsend Street, directly across from Sid's Market. The Koppelmans apartment building was on the corner of Townsend and Humboldt. Nobody white lived on Aleta's block of Humboldt. Nobody black lived on Townsend. The corners on which Marvin and Aleta's buildings stood were the dividing line between black and white.

The Koppelmans lived on the second floor and Aleta lived on the third, so Marvin and Aleta could look out of their windows at each other—not that they often did. And from her apartment window, Aleta could see and hear Mrs. Koppelman trailing Marvin around the block several times a week, bearing the silver cup like a standard before her.

Sometimes when Marvin came out to play, the other white kids who lived in the buildings lining Townsend Street wouldn't play with him. The black kids on Humboldt would, though. They'd chase him, yelling, "Come on, Marvinsky, drink your milk, or you won't grow up to be big and strong like Superman."

But that changed for Aleta on a day when she was sitting outside on her front steps, and Marvin came plodding along, followed by the usual group holding their hands in the air like a cup and yelling at him about his milk. Marvin's fat face was flushed a bright red. As he looked back over his shoulder at the little band of black kids, his eyes were bright and shiny and filled with joy, yet so fearful at the same time that a little tingle settled in Aleta's stomach. She looked away.

After that, Aleta stopped chasing Marvin. She wouldn't play with him at all. She just competed harder with him in school. He didn't compete back, though. He didn't even notice. Marvin never cared about how smart he was. He never seemed to care about much of anything, except that crazy game of his, making people chase him all the time. Aleta started to hate him.

One day when Aleta went outside and sat on the front steps— third from the bottom, her favorite spot, she spied Marvin. She'd been upstairs eating a bowl of corn flakes, which she'd gotten from Sid's Market right after school, along with a quart of milk. After the cereal and milk were in the bowl, Aleta noticed there was no sugar, but sugar was not on her mother's list of allowables to be charged. So she ate the cereal even though it didn't taste good; but there was nothing else to eat in the house. That morning, Mama had told Aleta to go to the store.

"Get what you need after school. Bread, milk, cereal."

"Mama, can I get some cookies?"

"Not today."

"Tomorrow?"

"Not tomorrow either. We can't afford it, you know that."

"Of course we can't, we can never afford anything. What's the use?"

"What do you mean, what's the use, girl? You see me going out here every day pulling these days' work to put food in your stomach, and you ask me *what the use is?*"

"Well, what food?" It's always the same thing. Why can't we have something good once in a while?"

"You go to Sid and get one loaf of bread, one quart of milk and one box of cereal, and not one other thing. I better not see extra things signed for in that book when I go to pay the bill tomorrow."

"I wasn't going to do that," Aleta muttered, looking at the floor.

"Well, you've done it before, haven't you?" Aleta didn't answer. "Well, haven't you?" she repeated.

"Yes!" Aleta shouted and began to stomp around her to get her coat. Mama caught her arm and held her still.

"You know Mama would do better if she could, don't you?" again, Aleta didn't answer.

"You'll have more when you're older and some of the bigger ones are out on their own. We have to make do and share what we have. You're not starving, you know. You just don't have extras. It will be better by and by. Go on, now, don't be late for school."

Mama's rough hand rested on her head for a moment, Mama's only form of caress.

Aleta's brother Ralphie was waiting for her downstairs in the hallway. "Listen, Aleta, I'll bring home some baloney when I get done tonight and tell Sid to take it out of my pay, okay?" She nodded; she didn't want to talk about it.

After school Aleta stopped across the street to get the things Mama had said. Actually, the Skerritt children had permanent permission to get bread, milk and cereal at Sid's anytime, without asking her. Aleta looked at the oranges and bananas, canned meat and all the other really tasty stuff, but they had to sign in the book for whatever they bought, and Mama had warned Aleta, so she knew she'd be checking.

Mrs. Skerritt owed Sid too much, and she wanted to be able to pay it all off this week because next week was rent. She always said that Sid was a really fair grocer. He didn't weigh his thumb on the scale along with the goods you were buying, he gave credit, and he didn't hound you—and he had his bills to pay too. Mama and the other parents around the neighborhood respected him. That meant none of the kids would swipe from Sid, like they did from some other store owners who cheated people and treated them like dirt.

So anyway, Aleta was just sitting on the steps promising herself that she'd never eat cold cereal again once she was grown, when she heard the neighborhood kids come running past. "Marvin, Marvinsky, hey blobbo Marvin, drink some milk or you'll be too skinny to stand up straight." Marvin was moving in his usual ugly fashion. His broad feet, laced into blocky brown shoes, barely lifted off the sidewalk and he expelled a short groaning whine with every other step. He turned his upper body to look back occasionally, which threw him off balance, adding a lurch to his gait. My brother's friend, Gus was laughing and chasing, looking over his shoulder, encouraging the others to follow. Eloise, Joyce and Mason were trooping along chanting *milk, milk, milk, milk,* keeping pace with Marvin, making sure not to close the gap. If they caught him, the game would be over.

"Oh, stop it, will you?" Aleta said. "Can't we find some game to play besides chasing after somebody who can't even run, and can't even keep his fights inside his own house?"

"Well, what's the matter with you, all of a sudden?" Eloise came to a stop at the foot of the stoop.

"Yeah, you were chasing him just the other day," said Mason.

"I was not."

"You were too, Aleta. I saw you."

"Me too, I saw you," said Eloise. "You were, Aleta, don't lie," other voices chimed in.

"That was *weeks* ago," Aleta said. "I haven't chased him in *weeks!*"

Marvin turned and came back to stand with the others.

"It's okay, Aleta, they're just playing. They're not hurting me," Marvin said, as if he was explaining some basic problem to an idiot.

"Then why are you making those noises like you're scared to death?" Aleta asked, as his mother leaned out the window and began yelling, "Marvin, come home, come on home, sweetheart, don't let them get you." That made Aleta really furious. Mrs. Koppelman hadn't said anything when they were chasing him. Now that he was standing still like a normal person, she starts yelling. What a family. The only one with any sense was Sid.

"If you're not scared, why are you acting like that, huh? Why?" By now Aleta was on her feet and in his face. He backed away, a faint gleam of fear flashing in his eyes.

"I *am* scared," he said. She advanced on him. "Just a little bit, though," he added quickly.

She pushed him. "What about now?" Aleta asked.

"A little bit more," he said, a tiny grin appearing at the corner of his mouth.

She shoved him into the wall, hard. "Now?" Aleta screamed at him. Her throat was beginning to hurt. "A little bit more? Huh? Are you a little bit more scared? Are you?"

Marvin tried to edge sideways. Aleta grabbed his shirt and yanked him toward her, then shoved him against the wall again.

Gus was yelling, "Hey, what's going on with you anyway, Aleta? I'm going to get Ralphie." He dashed across the street.

Aleta slapped Marvin on the side of his face as he tried to run. "*Now* you've got something to be afraid of!"

Marvin's mother was screaming from her window, "My boy, somebody help my boy, she'll kill him, oh, somebody please help him. Stop her, stop that crazy Schvartze, she's crazy, crazy!"

Now Marvin had turned and was running back toward his house. Running *for real*, picking up and putting down as hard as his tubby legs would go, not stopping once to look over his shoulder. Aleta ran behind, pounding on his back hearing her own words hurtling toward the back of his head. "Drink your milk, drink your milk, eat your food, you go to hell! You and your crazy mother . . . milk on the sidewalk. I'll kill you, *I'll kill you.*"

Suddenly, strong arms yanked her from behind and held her tight while Marvin sped down the street to cheers from the kids and mothers who gathered on the stoop of his apartment building, most of who had risen from their usual sitting positions. Behind Aleta there was shocked silence from her friends.

Sobbing and breathless, she was led upstairs by Ralphie and Gus, who never asked her what prompted the incident. Not that she'd have known what to tell them.

The following week, Aleta won the Spelling Bee for the girls, Thelma Kosciusko having turned out to be no real match for her after all. During the remainder of the spring and summer, none of the kids chased Marvin—nor did his mother. The next year, in sixth grade, Marvin challenged Aleta heads up in every subject. He even beat her in spelling. That was the year they changed it so there was only one top winner.

Roxbury 1950s

Bus Stop at 3:00 P.M.

Aleta saw him waiting at the bus stop from three blocks away, as she turned the corner. Just him alone. Waiting for her. Oh, no! Backing up two steps, easing around the corner just before he could catch sight of her, Aleta said to Ellen, "Come on, let's race up to Harrishof Street. I'll catch the bus there."

Ellen frowned, puzzled. "That's stupid. We're almost at the corner already. You always catch the bus here. What's the matter?"

"I don't know," Aleta answered, "I just feel like going up the street. Come on, Ellen, let's race." Taking a few steps to the corner, Ellen looked down the street at the man waiting by the bus stop, and then turned back to Aleta.

"Okay, let's go up Harold, and then we'll cross over at Harrishof to the bus stop on Humboldt, okay?" Ellen said.

"Right, that's it, let's go, then." They took off, black skinny legs flying, saddle shoes pumping up and down. Ellen ran with chin lifted, elbows pushing rhythmically and close to her sides. Aleta's head was tucked down, eyes watching the ground ahead while her chest leaned forward. They were each other's best challenge in running, reading, and playing the dozens.

As they approached the corner, they saw the bus appear from over the hill, racing toward them. Neck and neck, they picked up speed, dashing across Humboldt Avenue to the bus stop. The driver, seeing their determination, slowed down, timing his stop so that they all pulled up to the corner at the same moment.

Panting, Aleta fumbled in her pocket for her nickel as she climbed aboard. Then she heard Ellen's voice, close behind her ear, "You better tell your mother about that man!" Startled, Aleta paused with one foot on the step and looked back over her shoulder at Ellen, who stood on the sidewalk looking solemnly out of wise, city-girl eyes.

Frozen there, Aleta heard the driver's voice, "Alright, young lady, let's go. Folks waiting." She stepped inside the bus, dropped her nickel in the box, and walked down the aisle to an empty double seat.

As she side-stepped in, Aleta saw Ellen outside the open window. She had run alongside the bus and was now facing Aleta. "You better tell your mother, girl!" The bus took off abruptly, the seat knocking Aleta behind her knees, forcing her to plop down. Just as she sat, Aleta realized they were about to pass the corner where he always stood, in his shabby brown overcoat, hands deep in his pockets.

Yes, there he was, feet planted firmly in his rundown shoes. Behind him a laughing blonde with bright red lips took up half the drugstore window. "Drink Coca Cola," she urged. As the bus entered his line of vision, Aleta began sliding down in the seat but couldn't resist turning her head to see if he was looking. His cocoa brown face with the little stubble of grey and black beard was turned upward toward the bus window. As the bus rolled slowly past, Aleta peered at him and saw his soft brown eyes reproaching her.

She pulled herself erect in the seat, wondering if she was imagining things. After all, he hadn't said anything really wrong to her —not exactly. They rolled past her favorite neighborhood, a wide sweeping curve of pretty one-and-two-family houses: grey trimmed with white, brown trimmed with yellow, and white houses with low wooden or wire fences trimmed with roses. The side and front yards held apple trees, with flowering white buds and magnolias bursting with purple, pink and white blossoms. This was one of the most satisfying parts of her ride, especially in the spring, and Aleta took time out from her worrying to enjoy it. Whenever she was on the bus with someone and they passed this stretch, she always fell silent, even if she was in the middle of a conversation.

She reminded herself that this would likely be one of the last times she would make the ride through this particular part of Roxbury. She'd be in a new school next year—and who could tell what she'd have to look at along the way. When she and the other six girls from her school had gone to visit Girls' Latin, they had to take two buses and a streetcar. Their teacher, in explaining to them how to get there, had called it a trolley. Whenever Aleta let herself think about the new school, with the smartest kids from all over the city who'd be going there, she got a queasy little lurch in her stomach.

Aleta had always felt comfortable with the white kids in her school, even when they fought with each other, even when they called each other "nigger" or "white trash." The name-calling was so evenly matched that nobody felt especially upset about it. Besides, kids always ended up playing together again, sometimes right after they fought.

But there was something different about the white girls they'd been with at that "orientation" at Girls' Latin. For the first time, Aleta felt that she was among people who didn't really think she belonged. When Mama and the rest of the family asked how the orientation went, she'd said in her usual *I can handle anything* manner, "Fine. It was okay. I think I'll do just fine," knowing that she was lying.

Aleta and her brothers and sisters tried not to worry Mama, especially during this time. When they were small, they'd thought Mama was strong enough to take care of anything, but now, even though they didn't say it to each other, they weren't so sure. They kept their little worries to themselves and tried to go to Mama only if they had real emergencies.

Just this past Christmas, Aleta had realized, for the third year in a row, that she shouldn't ask Mama for a bicycle. It wasn't fair to keep asking for things that Mama couldn't give; it just made her feel bad. Twelve-year-old Ralphie, Aleta's elder by two years, had been working in a grocery store since he was ten. He didn't ask Mama for anything at all. Fourteen-year-old Lilly had been babysitting for three years, spending whatever money she earned at the movies. She spent so much time at the movies that they all teased her about it.

Aleta knew she couldn't work yet, but at least she could keep from adding to Mama's worries. Mama was always talking about how hard it was for a widow to bring up seven children by herself. Aleta had heard her say, probably a hundred times, "It's a struggle keeping a decent place for my children to live, but just any old place won't do. You have to live in decent surroundings. I can't bring you up around bums. If that's all you see, that's all you'll be."

So Mama worked two jobs, and sometimes the meals were pretty sparse, but she said she'd rather the family ate less so they could enjoy a piano, a record player, and steam—instead of coal-fired—heat. She said that if you know what it is to live in a good neighborhood, that's the way you'll always want to live.

That's why it was the shame of Mama's life when her struggles with the landlord ended up with the family being evicted.

None of the children knew just what the battles were about, but sometimes when Mama sent them down to the office on the first floor of their building, the landlord refused to take the rent from them. Then Mama would go storming down and come back upstairs with a receipt, saying that there were some hard people in this world who thought a woman with children didn't have a right to live. "I'm no grass widow. I had a husband who took care of his family," she'd say, "and a better man never lived. He had more decency in his little finger than that lousy thief downstairs—always talking about evicting people. A black man, too, treating other black people so mean." When he first began acting this way, Mama predicted that he was plotting to toss them out as soon as he legally could, so that he could split the large apartments into small ones and make more money. Two other families with children, one who had lived above them on the fourth floor and one below them on the second, had already been forced out.

The landlord finally succeeded. The children came home from school one day and found their belongings spread out on the sidewalk, their lives turned upside down. They were locked out of their apartment and had to wait outside for Mama to come home from work. While Ralphie and several neighborhood boys stood protectively around the edges of their stuff, Lilly stood defiantly proud, staring off down the street, refusing to look at anyone.

Their kitchen dishes and utensils and their laundry sat in boxes and bags on the sidewalk, surrounded by the couch, the dining room table and the kitchen chairs. The dark brown piano sat abandoned at the side of the doorsteps, its back to the sidewalk, like a child being put in the corner in kindergarten; the cover which was always opened was closed. On the kitchen table was piled all the old junk from the back of closets: odd pieces of clothing, a baseball glove, incomplete games, playing cards, books and toys. Every toy that had been missing in their large, comfortable home was sitting outside in a huge, mountainous mass. Peeking through the middle of the junk was the old baby doll with the broken off arm, the one that Lilly, Aleta and KayKay had all owned in turn. Lying on their sides were three broken straw baskets that had been filled with Easter candy several years ago.

Aleta's eyes travelled slowly until she spied what was once her favorite teddy bear, which she had named Josie. Only to herself, of course. None of them would ever admit to having a toy with a name— that would have been the source of too much teasing. Josie had been lost for years. Aleta had looked for her rather avidly for three years, and then gave up. Now, as Josie peered up at her with her one yellow glass eye, Aleta felt a big lump in her throat and tears in her eyes. She was so stunned with shame and loss that she ran down the street to the corner of their block and upstairs into her godmother's house and didn't come back out, not even to go to school, until Mama came to get her two days later.

While Aleta was with her godmother and KayKay with hers, the rest of the kids stayed with various friends. But then Mama came for them, and they all got to be together again. First they stayed in three rooms in a rooming house with a very nice woman. She lent them two hotplates to warm food on. They washed their dishes in the bathtub. Then Mama found what she called their "emergency" apartment. "We'll just have to make it do for one year. We can pull together and be strong. It's not anything like what you're used to, and I don't even want you to get used to it, but we'll clean it the best we can and try to stand it."

"But Mama, there's not enough rooms for us to have beds for everyone," piped up Aleta's younger sister, KayKay. The others shushed and nudged her to keep quiet, but Mama replied, "We'll have to sleep in new ways. This is only four rooms, not seven. But we can do it." Mama's voice was cheerful, but her eyes were so sad that Aleta looked at Ralphie, hoping he could say something to make Mama feel better. He could always make Mama laugh. "It's okay, Mama. I like it around here," he said. "It'll be fine for me." Aleta groaned inside. That's just what Mama was afraid of. The kind of kids outside were exactly who Mama had been trying to keep her kids away from. Aleta looked at Lilly, who was looking at Ralphie, one eyebrow cocked in disbelief.

When she'd first stepped inside the dingy, cramped little apartment, Lilly had looked around and said softly, almost to herself, "I can't stay here." Now, Lilly said, "Don't worry, Mama, I don't spend that much time around the house, between school and baby-sitting. Aleta has her reading and schoolwork to do, and you know KayKay hardly ever goes out when you're not home. We'll get along just fine."

And they did, in a way. Mama and Lilly slept on a pull-out couch in the living room. Ralphie slept in the kitchen on a cot, which he had to fold up and put away in the living room closet every morning. Aleta slept on a cot in the living room that stayed up all day with a cover over it, pretending to be a sofa. KayKay slept in the dark, tiny back room. Nineteen-year-old Julie, the oldest sister, studying in secretarial school, stayed with her best friend in the South End and came to visit only once or twice a week, and then she slept with KayKay. Where fastidious Lilly was repulsed by their new home, Julie was deeply ashamed. She wanted to leave secretarial school and get a job to help the family get into a better place, but Mama said, "No." Everyone had to stay in school so their lives would be better someday in the future.

In spite of her struggles, Mama ended up "losing our whole past"—which wound up incarcerated in storage—because she couldn't keep up the payments on the furniture and pay rent for their new apartment too. That's when she was the saddest the children had ever seen her. For months, it seemed like she didn't laugh or joke or sing around the house, or bake bread as she used to do in their beautiful old apartment. Julie told them that was because some of the things lost were precious from her years with Daddy. This included her wedding dress and the elegant brass bed that had been their wedding gift to themselves, and where all the children except one had been born.

In this "one-year apartment" on Gertrose Street, from the kitchen, you looked right into the living room, with no door as separation. The Gertrose Street apartment opened directly from the outside hall either into a dingy, dark kitchen without windows or directly into a living room with two narrow windows that looked out over the grim, hopeless street, where children ran up to the backs of the wagons, and grabbed handfuls of shaved ice that tumbled down as the drivers chipped off a 25 or 50-cent block with ice-picks. The children shoved the ice into their mouths after picking out the tiny pieces of black coal embedded in the slivers. Ralphie could grab a handful, shove it in, spit out the black pieces and chew on the ice without blinking an eye. He was getting so tough since they moved over this way. If Ralphie had been like his old self, Aleta might have told him about the man at the bus stop and they could have figured something out, like their old way of handling things.

Well, the old days were gone, Aleta told herself, standing up as the bus pulled into Dudley station. Aleta had to admit to herself that she was just plain scared about the man, so maybe she'd better just go ahead and tell Mama about him. Besides, Mama always said, "I have a job to do, raising you children. When Daddy died, it was all up to me . . . and nobody's going to walk all over my children while there's breath in my body." So it just stood to reason that if Aleta tried to handle it herself and something bad happened, Mama would feel like she had failed to do her proper job. Aleta nodded to herself firmly. That was it. She wasn't equipped to handle it herself. Mama had to know. As she walked up to the front to get off the bus, she heard a gruff voice.

"Hey, young lady."

"Yes?" She turned her head to look back at the driver.

"You sure can run," he said, giving her a broad smile.

"Thanks," Aleta said, forcing a little smile back at him.

When Aleta got home, she waited impatiently for Mama. Having decided to tell her, Aleta already felt almost free of the man. When Mama and KayKay came up the stairs, Aleta took the shopping bags from her and set them on the floor, shifting from foot to foot as Mama shucked her coat. As KayKay walked back toward her bedroom, Mama asked, "Something wrong?"

Aleta blurted, "mama, there's a man . . ."

As she reached for the coat hook on the wall behind the door, Mama's arm stopped in mid-air. She looked over her shoulder at Aleta, who looked back into Mama's piercing dark eyes, nestled between protruding, sharp cheekbones and prominent low brows. "Some man bothering you? Where?" she asked as she turned from the wall and began walking into the living room.

Aleta followed. "Near my school. He waits for me at the bus stop."

Mama sat on the cot that doubled as Aleta's bed. "And what does he say? Here, sit down. Tell me everything." Once Aleta began talking, the words came eagerly, propelled along by Mama's involvement. It was a relief to let Mama take over and extract the story from her.

"He asks me to go to his house with him."

"Why?"

"He says he wants me to clean up his dishes for him and he'll pay me."

"Did you tell him you don't want to?"

"Yes. But he keeps bothering me. He knows what time I get out of school, and now he's there every day at the bus stop."

"You scared of him?" "Yes, Mama."

"What else?"

"He's always offering me money for candy. When I say no, he says he'll give me my bus fare then I can use my own money for candy. That way I'm not taking candy from a strange man. Then he laughs." Mama's lips pressed so tight together that they disappeared inside her mouth. "Does he touch you?"

"Yes, he kind of crowds in on me and keeps putting his hands on my face and touching my shoulders."

"Humph," Mama said. She was silent for a long few minutes, "I'm going to send for your brothers. This man needs to be made to leave you alone, and I mean *quick*! We've got to make plans. Now, let's get supper started."

After supper, Mama sent Ralphie to find the oldest two boys, Wesley and Alan, who lived separately in rooming houses somewhere in the South End, not very far from the family's Roxbury apartment. Wesley, who was 21, always let Mama know when he moved, and he could be counted on to keep tabs on Alan, the second-born, a year and a half younger. Within two hours, both Wesley and Alan were there, along with Cousin Bobby, who was also around their age, and who everyone said might just as well be Mama's son too. Bobby's mother died when he and his sister were young and their aunt had raised them (and spoiled them, Mama always said). Wesley, Alan, and Bobby gathered in the small living room, with Mama and Aleta on the cot. Alan sat on the couch beside Cousin Bobby, who kept rubbing his hands together and looking from one to the other of the boys. "Sheez, we gotta get this guy. An old guy like that, he should be ashamed. We oughta knock his head off." Alan cut in with his staccato stutter, "Gotta...gotta...gotta...be...c...c...crazy bothering a little girl."

"Quiet, now," said Wesley, who had pulled a kitchen chair into the living room. "Just let her talk. I want to hear everything." As he listened, the only sign of Wesley's anger was the pulsing of his jaw as he clenched his teeth over and over. He sat erect, looking intently at Aleta, ready to draw out the story in his careful, teacherly manner. Wesley knew how to get the facts. That was his way. Now he said, "When did he first start talking to you?"

As Aleta gave more details of her meetings with the man, she realized how frightened she had been for the past few weeks. They continued talking for about two hours, and even though they asked all kinds of specific questions, she wasn't embarrassed. Everybody calmed down and acted as if they were simply there to find the solution to a problem. Aleta answered everything as clearly as she could.

Then, plotting together, all of them—including Mama—came up with the plan. They went over it several times until there could be no doubt that Aleta knew her part. The only problem she had with the plan was the need to rely so completely on her brothers. All her life she had heard Mama telling off the boys, especially Wesley, the oldest, for not being reliable. So it wasn't Mama or the plan that she didn't trust. But the brothers? All night long, Aleta couldn't sleep. All night long, she kept going over and over her part, hoping and praying that the boys would come through.

The next day, the hands of the clock on the schoolroom wall inched their way to 3:00 p.m. Aleta hadn't heard a thing from the moment she had entered at 8:30 that morning. She pledged allegiance and sang the national anthem; she looked at the other students and at Miss Owens; she saw their mouths moving: she opened books and wrote on papers; she acted the same way as always, but she felt as if she were inside a huge vacuum bottle where no sound could penetrate. She rubbed her clammy hands repeatedly on her skirt. She longed for a drink of cold water to slide down her throat, which felt like it was stuck together with glue. Her eyes kept sneaking peeks at the clock, as it raced and crept all at once. The constant chatter in her head said: *Will they be there? Will they remember? Should I just run the other way? If I don't go, what will happen?*

Aleta heard desktops slamming all around her and realized that her classmates were putting away books and papers, preparing to finish for the day. She began doing the same, and as she did, her thoughts switched to Ellen. She didn't want to deceive her best friend, but Mama had said no one was to know. *No one,* she'd said, looking intently at Aleta with that special, penetrating stare. Aleta had promised that no one would. So now, on top of everything else, she had to plot how she was going to avoid Ellen.

Finally the 3 o'clock bell rang, propelling Aleta into her place in the double line forming at the door: next to last in the girls' line. She felt herself shifting from side to side, eager to be on the move. Her head was pounding and she had to keep pushing her glasses back up on her sweaty nose. Then the second bell rang, the front door of the school opened, and the children filed sedately out the door, only to burst apart when they got to the corner, flying in all directions and yelling loudly. Aleta was yelling too as she ran wildly down the street, in fear of what was coming, and pretending she didn't hear Ellen way back in her line, calling Aleta's name. She had decided she couldn't let Mama down; she had to give the plan her all. Everyone was in it because of her, so she would just have to do her part and trust.

As she came in sight of the bus stop, Aleta slowed down, walking at a normal pace towards him. When he looked up and saw her coming, a huge smile spread all over his face. For a fleeting second, Aleta felt ashamed of the trick she was about to play. She concentrated on walking steadily forward and trying to keep her face looking natural.

"Well, hello there. I was beginning to think you didn't like me anymore," he said, kind of rolling the words around in his throat, sounding the way she imagined a giant panda would.

"What do you mean?" she asked.

"You've stopped coming this way. I was about to walk on up to Harrishof Street and check if you might be coming that way," he said slyly, making sure she knew that he'd seen her go by on the bus yesterday. Aleta's stomach crawled. He'd said just the right words to help her get over feeling ashamed for tricking him. She could almost feel her shoulders squaring off, and had to restrain herself from reaching down to pull up her socks, which were always slipping down into her scuffed saddle shoes.

"No, sometimes I walk that way with my friend but I'm by myself today."

"Well, I missed you yesterday. You want some money for candy? Oh, I forgot. You want some money for the bus?" Aleta just kept looking at him. His eyes ran up and down her skinny body. She could feel him getting up the courage to ask the same old question again. He was so sure she'd say no that he probably just asked it out of habit to give himself a laugh. "You'd be earning your own money. Few minutes, it'd be yours. Your mother wouldn't even have to know you did it."

"Did what?" Aleta asked. His pink tongue licked out between his dark lips, while his nostrils flared quickly. Twice. "Uh...uhn, my dishes, and there's a few other things you could do around the house."

"Oh, all right. You show me what to do, though. O.K?"

"What, what? You'll come? Oh, yes, yes, I'll show you. Come on then, come on."

He was so excited that he took her elbow and began rushing her up the street towards his house, one of a group of three-story, red brick buildings in the middle of the block across Humboldt Avenue, only two blocks from "back home." Aleta's heart was pounding so hard in her chest, she thought he must be able to hear it. Her knees were trembling so much she couldn't walk fast enough to keep up with him. The sun was shining down from such a perfect blue sky that she just knew God wouldn't let her die on such a gorgeous day. As they crossed the street to head into his apartment building, Aleta wouldn't turn her head to look because she had promised not to, but her eyes were flying right, left, up and down the street, trying to catch a glimpse of her family of men. They had to be around here somewhere. *Please, Please, Please. . . Be here somewhere or he's going to do something awful to me!*

He could feel her resistance, and started talking in a low murmur, "Don't be afraid, little girl, it's going to be all right. I'll take care of you, treat you just fine. Don't worry, don't be afraid, everything's going to be all right." As Aleta and the man entered the hallway, the inner doors crashed back against the wall so hard that she could see the glass trembling in the frame, and there they were, all three of them. They yanked the man into the hallway, and Aleta heard their fists smacking against his flesh. "No, oh, please. Oh, no, stop, don't hurt me," he pleaded, his voice quaking, just as her knees had been shaking a few minutes earlier. Only grunts came from Aleta's protectors as they ignored the man's pleas and pounded him. But, peering through her fingers, Aleta noticed that Alan wasn't doing any hitting.

The man wriggled free, pushed open his first-floor apartment door and rushed inside, trying to close it behind him. Bobby said. "Aw, no you don't," holding the door easily with one hand while the man turned and fled, flinging open the bathroom door, diagonally across from the front door. Now Aleta could hear him vomiting into the toilet. She was crouching against the stairs in the outside hallway, fists clenched against her ears, when Alan came out of the apartment looking for her. With a gentle, "Aw, c-co-come here, honey," he reached out and pulled her close. Aleta pushed her head hard into his chest, waiting for the sounds to subside. Then, somehow, they were all crowded inside his apartment, Alan and Aleta right outside the bathroom, Bobby and Wesley inside, where the man sat on the toilet with his pants down around his ankles on the floor, snuffling up the tears running down his face as he looked up at them.

Alan, Aleta's peaceful second brother, just kept holding her close to his side, watching the action as he tried to shield his little sister from seeing the man sitting on the toilet. But the bathroom door was wide open, and she was looking at his reflection through the open door in the mirror above the tub. The stench of his loosened bowels turned Aleta's stomach, and she concentrated on not retching. Bobby and Wesley were outdoing one another as they told him how they felt about him bothering little girls. Then Aleta heard him pleading. "No, no . . . that's not it. See, I just wanted her to do some chores for me."

"Shut up," Wesley said, his words cold and chopped. "Don't insult our intelligence." He reached over almost casually from where he sat on the side of the tub and delivered a sharp, even-handed slap. The man's head rocked, and Aleta heard him whisper, "O.K., yes, sir." he smiled a hideous grin as tears poured down his face. Aleta shoved her face harder into Alan's chest.

Then she heard Wesley saying calmly, "Aleta. Aleta. Look at me." She turned her head slowly toward Wesley. "You have to *look* at him. This is the dirt that's out on these streets. You have to *look at him*. You always have to look at dirt like this, so they know you know them. You did just right, telling us about him. Now look at him. He's just dirt, see? See?" Aleta nodded. Wesley started talking to the man again. "Take a good, long look at this child so you can know that if you ever see her anywhere in your vicinity, you'd better cross the street, turn a corner, or find some way to disappear. You understand me?" *His head bobbed slowly.* "I don't ever want her to have to see your face again. Got that?" *His head bobbed faster.* "You'd better make sure you stay out of her way, because if she ever sees you, even by accident, you're in trouble." *He whimpered softly.* "And we'd better not hear any stories about other little girls around town either. We're going to be watching you carefully, man. You know what I mean, don't you?" His head bobbed up and down repeatedly while he whimpered. Aleta couldn't help feeling sorry for him. She wondered if the brothers noticed how pitiful he looked. They left him there, sitting on the toilet, moaning over and over, "Oh, my God. Oh, my God."

All the way home the brothers kept chuckling about the shocked look on the guy's face, and congratulating Aleta on how well she had done her part. She never remembered to ask them how they knew which hallway was his since Aleta had never known herself.

Months later, Aleta asked Mama how the boys knew which hallway was his. Mama laughed. "Did you forget your brothers spent their lives in that neighborhood? Wesley asked you plenty about that man when we talked that night, didn't he?" Aleta nodded. "He probably found out before he even went to sleep who the man was.

What was difficult for you or me would be no trouble at all for him," she said proudly. When Aleta told her how scared she had been that the brothers wouldn't show, Mama was surprised. "I wish I had known. You didn't have to worry, you know."

"But why, Mama? You're always fussing at them about not being responsible."

"Well, it's true that you can't count on them for everything. But for something like this, the only way they wouldn't be there is if they were dead."

"All of them?"

"Yes, but especially Wesley. He's always thought of himself as the man of the house since Daddy died. Now, it's true, he doesn't take all his responsibilities seriously. But for some things, I'd bet my life he'd be there," she said softly.

"Like what things?" Aleta asked, beginning to understand, but wanting more.

"Like looking after their sisters out in these streets. That's the main thing they can do for you children that I can't. And they must do that. They *must*. If they don't, they can't come to me anymore."

"Did you tell them that?"

"They know."

"How?" There was a little pause as Aleta looked up into the all-knowing pools of Mama's dark eyes, waiting.

"They just know," Mama said softly. "They just know."

Carol Leader of the Pack

They'd never belong here! Not Mama, not her sisters, nor Aleta. She didn't really want to belong anyway. She *hated* it here. Her brother Ralphie, fit right in from day one. He ran around with the other boys, chasing after the trucks that sold fruit in the streets, swiping stuff off of them and racing up the alley to the common yard that ran behind the block of apartment buildings on Gertrose Street, where they divvied up the loot and planned their next marauding attack.

Lilly had a babysitting job and came home only to sleep. KayKay, stayed at her godmother's across town after school, and Mama stopped by to pick her up—along with daily groceries—on her way home from work at six o'clock. Aleta, ten, had been trying to fit in since last April, when they first moved to Gertrose Street. Now it was August and she was glad to be going back to school in a few weeks. Of course, she would never reveal that to the other girls on the block, whose only discussion about school was to express delight when they had a day off.

In spite of her shyness, Aleta had tried hard to make friends with Carol, Delores, Sylvie, and the few other girls on her block, but they didn't ever seem to really play. Not in the way the girls did back on Humboldt Ave., the other part of Roxbury, where on any given day, they would move among several different activities in the space of a few hours: jump rope, dodge ball, jacks, word games, roller skating, roaming in Harold Park, sitting around on the stoop outside or in their houses, teasing each other, going to Saturday "triple movie days," where they saw a cowboy movie, a funny one (Laurel & Hardy or The Three Stooges), and a few cartoons.

And racing! Aleta almost always won, against both girls and boys, whether it was a short sprint from one end of the block to the other, a long one, up to the bus stop two blocks away, and back, or the "big race" that took five minutes, all the way around the long, wide and sunny block of Humboldt. The big one was the only race that Aleta had ever lost, so it was the one that the kids, and even some adults, would sometimes bet on—licorice sticks, gum balls, pickles, trading cards, and sometimes even their best marbles. She had lost the "big race" twice, each time because she got a stitch in her side: once to her brother Ralphie, which made it almost okay to lose, and once to his friend Gus, which bothered her a lot more. That's the kind of fun they used to have, while streetcars or buses moved along the wide avenues, transporting neighbors, parents, and children. But in this strange excuse for a neighborhood, only the boys played hard— running, laughing and having fun—while the girls waited, hanging around this one short block on Gertrose, with its eight identical apartment houses staring directly across at eight others exactly like them, glaring straight back.

The buildings, three stories high, blocked the sunlight for most of the daytime hours, except for a brief period in early afternoon when the sun sat at its zenith, desperately begging for attention. At other times of the day, patches of sunlight managed occasionally to show up as slim panels on the sidewalks, slipping slyly between whichever buildings were separated by narrow spaces. Women hung out of stingy, narrow windows, conversing loudly with others across the way or out on the sidewalk. Or they leaned further out and twisted their heads sharply sideways to discuss with someone next door the paltry activities taking place up and down the block as they awaited the fish man, the rag man, the ice man, or the door-to-door insurance man.

Mama said she was "praying to God for strength and working like the devil" to get the family out of there.

It took very little time and no effort to figure out who was the leader of the girls on the block. Carol lived right across the street from Aleta, and directed all of the girl activities, mainly gathering on doorsteps, telling jokes, and deciding which girls were supposed to like which boys. Sometimes, while the ice and coal delivery truck was stopped in the street, they' scoop of slivered ice from the tail of the truck and slip it into their mouths. One time, Aleta tried it, but couldn't stand the taste or the tiny grits of coal that crunched in her teeth at unexpected moments. Carol laughed, calling her "picky," but Aleta didn't believe she was the only girl who didn't like it. She thought they were just copying the boys, who would, on the run, throw a casual handful of ice into their mouths and never take notice of any coal they might be crunching.

The girls wrote notes to the boys, an activity directed by Carol, who dictated what the notes should say. Then she sent certain girls as emissaries' to deliver the messages. After, they would put their heads together, and Carol would suggest notes that said things like, "I want to see you later." "Who do you like?" and "Do you like to kiss?" They folded the notes and dropped them out of Carol's second floor window, calling to the boys as they sped by on their bikes. Or they slipped them into the hands of the boys who were playing "kick the can" or "red rover" in the street. Or the emissary would run by the stoop or up the alley where the boys were hanging out, and drop a handful of notes with names pencilled on the outside, while the other girls cheered her back to the stoop, giggling and waiting to ask if any of the boys had said anything. Aleta wondered if they thought this was fun, or just didn't know what else to do.

The one activity that the boys and girls engaged in together was walking to the Woolworth's or Kresge's near Dudley Street station to swipe things. They'd do only one store, never two on the same day. It didn't matter what they took—candy, pads of paper, toys, or comic books—since it was only a pastime. Then they'd return home to share the loot at one of the two apartments where the parents were out working. Aleta and Ralphie's place was popular because Mama was gone all day and trusted them to be on their own until she got home. Aleta didn't let on, but she was ashamed whenever the kids came over, mainly because of their cots—Ralphie's, that he brought in from the kitchen, where he slept at night, and pushed into the living room closet in the morning; and her own, covered with a faded pink spread, trying to resemble a day bed as it stood catty-cornered to the couch, which pulled out into a double bed, where Mama slept (and Lilly, whenever she came home, which was seldom). KayKay slept in a tiny room behind the kitchen that Aleta firmly believed must have been a pantry before.

Aleta didn't know if Ralphie even noticed or cared about the way they lived now. Didn't he miss the space in their seven-room apartment with four bedrooms, a dining room, back porch and wide windows (bay windows, Mama called them) curving out in the living room, windows they helped Mama wash every couple of months with newspaper and vinegar? Only the insides though because they lived on the third floor. Aleta wondered if Ralphie missed the fun they used to have when it rained outside and they stayed inside playing jacks and pickup sticks and cards, and aggies and checkers and Chinese checkers, and dominoes and cops and robbers, and pulled each other in the little wagon up and down the long, wide hallway from the living room to the dining room, and pushed chairs together and threw blankets over them to make tents? Didn't he miss that?

Since they knew all the families with children in their old neighborhood, just stepping outside always brought some kind of adventure. Aleta and Ralphie had always been the closest two back then, but soon after they moved over to this part of the city, Aleta had to admit to herself that he wasn't interested in talking with her about anything anymore. They'd never mentioned their sadness about having to live in this dingy, cramped, hopeless little apartment, on this dreadful street, in this disgusting part of Roxbury.

Aleta had to constantly make herself *not cry* whenever she thought about it because she knew Mama was even sadder, although she tried not to show it. All her decent furniture, their good rugs, and their piano were in storage and Mama couldn't get them out. The beautiful brass bed that she and Daddy bought together as their own wedding gift was stored away. Even though Mama had to work two jobs after he died, she had always prided herself on continuing to bring them up just as she and Daddy had been doing: in the "good" part of Roxbury, in a steam-heated apartment with radiators and central heat, where there were decent schools and a variety of families of all backgrounds, including northern and southern blacks, Caribbean's, white immigrants from Ireland, Germany, and Poland, and Jews who had occupied that area for decades, but were gradually moving away.

Aleta never doubted that Mama would fulfill her promise to get them out of this place that she called "only a stop along the way." The way *to where?* Aleta thought, wondering if their family could ever be connected again, especially since no one ever talked about how awful it felt, how horribly scary. Would they ever get back to the way they had been with each other? How the others were thinking about this situation mystified Aleta. Only Lilly had commented at all.

Ralphie was running the streets with boys he wouldn't even have known in their previous neighborhood. KayKay's godmother took care of her after school. Poor Mama was trying hard to find a way to get them out of this nightmare. Aleta felt distinctly alone.

Although she was absolutely bored with the street, Aleta liked to go inside Carol's house, mainly because of Carol's mother, whose eyes smiled along with her mouth, and who always called Aleta Wise Owl. "Why so solemn, Miss Wise Owl?" she'd laugh, putting her fingers under Aleta's chin and tilting her face up. Whenever she said it, Aleta was reminded of how much more serious she had become these past few months, ever since they'd been evicted and had to end up living on this dingy little piece-of-a-street. Back home, which was how she always thought about their old apartment on Humboldt, she used to laugh and tease and make up wild stories which made her mother say, as the corners of her mouth turned up, "You can really spin them out, you know." Or, "Girl, stop your mouth, who you think can believe that nonsense?" in her melodious West Indian lilt that let Aleta know it was okay to tell tall tales and act silly.

Carol's mother was a curvy woman, the color of ginger snaps, and tall like Mama, but a lot younger. She had two boyfriends: Al, who was about her own age, and Tim, who was much older. Aleta thought he might be about fifty because he had grey hair mixed into his black, like Mama's, and Mama had said she'd be fifty in two years. Tim gave Carol money whenever she wanted, sometimes even without her asking for it, and when he came to the house he always brought bags of food and liquor. Carol's mother would say, "I like to have my drinks, I *must* say." Then she'd throw her head back and laugh, her shoulders and bosom shaking. She didn't work, and sometimes during the day she'd play cards or Chinese checkers with Carol and Aleta.

Carol's mother had a gray cat with white paws named Suzy-Q, who was free to jump onto her broad lap any time. She would stroke the cat and say, "Suzy-Q gonna be a mommy? Suzy-Q gonna have her some babies?" After a while, Suzy-Q had four kittens, one completely gray, one gray with white paws just like herself, one white, and one black— soft, stumbling, furry balls that Aleta paid little attention to, being as awkward around animals as she was around babies. Carol and her mother would pick up one or another, cradling it tenderly as they held it up to their faces, nuzzling it and saying, "Oh, isn't it just so soft and sweet? Isn't it just so adorable?" in tiny baby voices, looking at Aleta for a response. She'd nod, embarrassed at hearing it, and at herself for not knowing how to use such words. Carol's mother's eyes laughed into hers as if she knew what Aleta was thinking, while Suzy-Q prowled around their ankles, protective and watchful, until they put the kitten down, whereupon she'd pick it up and languidly take herself and her offspring into the hall closet where she'd birthed them.

One afternoon when Aleta was playing cards with Carol and her mother, she went to the bathroom and, as she was re-entering the kitchen, one— gray fuzzy kitten was just coming through the doorway toward her, nudged along by Suzy-Q, who held the black one dangling from her mouth. The other gray kitten, Suzy-Q's lookalike, trailed behind. Carol and her mother said at the same moment, "Look out!" as the little cat family made their way toward her. Aleta, backing up quickly into the hall as they came pushing past, felt a soft crunch under her foot. She lifted her foot and heard a squeal and a soft thump behind her. Suzy-Q dropped her black bundle and screeched out a loud *meyowl*, streaking past Aleta, who turned around to see the white kitten whimpering against the wall. Aleta screamed. Carol let out a long moan. Her mother said, "Oh, God!" The kitten, its eyes slowly turning red, staggered in a blind circle as Aleta stared, both hands pressed over her mouth, forcing her screams and her nausea inside. Suzy-Q, mewling pitifully, circled the white kitten a few times, then, gathering the rest of her offspring, walked them slowly into the closet and nudged the door shut. Carol's mother picked up the white kitten, which was shaking and drooping.

Aleta whispered, "Is it going to die?" Carol's mother nodded, wide dark eyes moving from the kitten to Aleta and back again. Hot tears spilled down the faces of both girls as Carol moaned and chanted,

"Oh, no, Ma. My favorite, Snowbaby. Oh, no, Ma, not Snowbaby. Oh, Ma . . ."

"Carol, please, baby, stop. Oh, Aleta, don't cry, honey, it's not your fault, you couldn't help it." She was starting to cry herself, pacing up and down the hall. "Carol, get me a jacket or something, hurry up, baby."

"Why? Where you going? You taking her to the hospital?" Carol yelled, rushing to snatch a sweater off the peg in the hall.

"No, no, never mind, I'll be back in a little while."

"Ma, don't let her die. Is she dying?"

"Baby, she's almost gone. Just stay here, I'll be back soon. Aleta, it's okay, honey, it was just an accident. Please don't suffer so, girl, everything's going to be all right."

She left the house, cradling the kitten in her arms, blood oozing from its ears and seeping into the arm of her light blue sweater. Soon after she left, Aleta started for the door. Carol came and hugged her from behind. Aleta turned around and hugged her in turn, both of them trembling with sorrow. Crossing the street and climbing the stairs to the second floor, Aleta went straight to the bathroom and crouched on the laundry bag in the corner, hugging herself tight and rocking, trying to wipe it all away, trying to make it not real. When she came to the supper table, she couldn't eat, a rare occurrence for her, but nobody noticed, for which she was glad. She didn't mention the kitten. That night, with Mama sleeping on the pull-out couch in the living room— Lilly beside her, on one of her rare nights with the family— Aleta lay absolutely still, clutching the sides of her cot, battling the swirling images that refused her an escape into sleep—spinning kitten . . . tears . . . moans . . . meyowling . . . redness on white fur. . . crunch of soft bone underfoot.

She and Carol never mentioned the incident, and they continued being friends, but Aleta didn't visit her at home again. Carol was still boss of the block, the girl with the stunning personality, which Aleta figured she'd inherited from her mother. There was no question that the girls liked Carol best. The boys didn't though. They knew who led the girls, but none of them sent Carol notes, or flipped her skirt as they ran by, or teased her the way they did the rest of the girls, including Aleta. Aleta never could understand what boys liked in girls anyway. If she was a boy picking a girlfriend, Carol would be first on her list.

In late August, shortly before returning to school, as the two friends sat on the steps in front of Aleta's building, Carol asked, "Does Ralphie ever say anything about me?"

"No, Ralphie never says anything to me about anything anymore."

"Did he use to?"

"Yeah, we were the two who always played together, from the time we were little. He used to be a lot more fun before we moved over this way."

"Well, of course you were younger then. I guess he likes to play more with boys now."

"I guess."

"Does he like me, do you think?"

"Why, do you like him?"

"Maybe."

"I thought you liked Davey."

"I used to, but you know he likes you now. You like him too, don't you?"

"I don't know, I guess so. I just like them all okay. You know, the same. All of them the same."

"Well then, how come you write him notes?"

"Just to do something, like you said. I don't know, you said I should write him, so I just did it. But I don't care if you want to start writing him again. I don't care, honest. Go ahead."

"No, I'm through with him. He's a baby anyway. So, listen, just ask Ralphie if he likes me, okay? Act like you're just curious."

"I'd feel funny. Why don't you just write, and I'll give him the note."

"Well, if you don't want to ask him, I guess I just might have to. Don't look at it, though."

"Oh, come on. Who do you think I am—Delores?" They laughed.

When Aleta gave Ralphie the note, she saw him huddling over it with his buddies and snickering. Then they all went into Davey's house. The next day she said, "Carol, don't bother with Ralphie and them. Let's us girls form our own club and think of things to do."

"Don't bother with them? Why?"

"They're getting too fresh. My mother says Ralphie is starting to think about nothing but looking up girls' dresses, and she's going to give him a good slap pretty soon."

"All boys do that. My mother says it's natural when you reach a certain age. You ought to know that."

"Maybe, but I guess my mother doesn't think he should be at that age yet."

"Well, I think Ralphie's pretty grownup for his age, just like me." Aleta didn't answer.

Later on, at home, Ralphie gave her a note. "Give this to Carol, and don't you dare look inside."

"Oh, give it to her yourself." Aleta flung it to the floor. "Just leave me out of it."

For the next couple of weeks, notes flew back and forth between Carol and Ralphie, carried by Delores or Sylvie. As school began, Carol and the rest of the girls were giving the cold shoulder to Aleta, who didn't know why but was feeling distinctly lonely and also relieved. She immersed herself in her homework and began staying longer at school and bringing home more library books.

One day when she came home and started up the stairs, she found Sisco and Davey sitting on the top step, directly in front of the door to her apartment that led into the living room. Whichever way she moved, they seemed to shift also, blocking her way. "Move," she said. They sat, silent. Her voice rose, "Hey, what's wrong with you? Move out of my way. This is *my* house, you know!" as she pushed past them. Shoving her way into the living room past two more boys, "And this is my room you're in, too, whether you know it or not."

There was a quick bustle of activity as Ralphie scrambled up off her cot, but not before she'd seen his skinny, bare behind wriggling around, his pants down around his ankles, with Carol's feet, encased in shiny red loafers, crossed in the air above his back. The other boys were hurriedly zipping up their pants and tucking their shirts in as Cisco and Davey crowded in from the stairway. Guilty faces swarmed around her, heads swiveling, eyes darting. Aleta heard her own voice rasping, shouting, "Ralphie, what do you think you're doing, you stinking rat!" He looked at her over his shoulder, his eyes closing for a long, anguished moment then re-opening as he turned his back, rising to his knees and reaching one hand behind him, groping clumsily for his pants.

Aleta approached the cot. "Come on, Carol," she said, reaching out her hand, trying to ignore the part of her brain that was screaming at her not to touch Carol's hand, the hand that must have touched the boys down there, each one of them, down there. Aleta wondered how she did it; did she have to touch their thing to put it in her? Aleta kept reaching past Ralphie, knowing that once Carol touched her hand, she'd be washing it for the next month— at least. She swallowed firmly, willing her stomach not to betray her by throwing up.

Ignoring Aleta's hand, Carol sat up, reached to the floor beside the cot to pick up her white cotton underpants, and turned sideways to put them on. Then, planting her red loafers firmly on the floor, she stood tall, pulled her panties up with a firm snap of the elastic waistband, straightened her dress, and turned to stare Aleta coldly in the eyes.
"Come on where? Where're you taking me, to the *library*? Just mind your own damn business, why don't you?"

"Yeah, mind your business," came a voice behind her "You think you're so smart, but you don't know anything" said another. "Keep your mouth shut, Miss Priss." "Miss know-it-all." "Ugly four-eyes."
The boys' taunts continued bouncing around the room, but when Carol opened her mouth, all sound receded, except for Carol's low-pitched voice, which entered on an exclusive private line, flat and purposeful, straight into Aleta's brain: "You don't know how to have fun. All you know how to do is *read*, clumsy-oaf-cat killer." Aleta's eyes locked with Carol's. Deep within Carol's eyes, Aleta saw them hugging each other in pain the night she killed Snowbaby. Could Carol see the same scene reflected in her eyes? Aleta heard the boys' voices continue, "Miss Latin School Genius." "Boney Maroney Phony." "Stuck-up Suck-up."

Then she heard Ralphie shouting above the din, "Stop! Leave her alone, alright? Just stop it!"

The room went quiet.

Carol pulled her gaze from Aleta's and moved in a mocking, womanly saunter toward the door. Then Ralphie, in his regular voice, with only a slight quaver floating beneath, said, "Come on, let's get out of here. Let's . . . just . . . go." They trooped silently out the door, Carol first, then the boys, followed by Ralphie.

Aleta stood looking at her cot.

Ralphie stuck his head back through the door and whispered, "Sorry, Aleta."

She couldn't move.

"Aleta?"

Slowly, she raised her eyes from the pink bed cover, now rumpled and stained.

"Sorry," he said again.

Aleta nodded, aware that she was looking between, not into, his eyes.

Ralphie turned away and rushed down the stairs. She felt a breeze blow through the door into the living room and drift delicately across her body as he flung open the downstairs door, bouncing it back against the wall in his haste.

Through the open living room window, Aleta heard Ralphie calling after them as he raced up the street "Wait, you guys; hey, wait!"

Humboldt Ave. & Townsnd St.

Let the Games Begin

Aleta wasn't really a great hitter, but she could run so fast that whenever she hit what would normally be an "out" for most of the boys she played with, she generally turned it into at least a single. And if the guys on the other team weren't used to playing with her, she might get a double out of it—because as soon as the bat connected, she took off, and when she reached first base, she would barely touch it, then pick up speed, her skinny black legs and arms pumping hard. The guys were so surprised that they almost always threw the ball too late to beat Aleta to second. So, even though she was the only girl who regularly played stickball with them, she was always chosen second or third when they picked teams.

Aleta's family had recently moved to Allegheny Street, where Aleta felt comfortable being able to play with girls and boys all mixed together—just like it had been during all her growing up years before they had spent that one horrible year on Gertrose Street, which she hoped she'd never see again.

None of the other girls in their twelve-to-fourteen-year-old crowd enjoyed playing stickball, but they didn't mind if Aleta did, just as long as she continued playing the rest of their other street games. When they weren't playing stickball, the guys joined the girls in games of kick-the-can, dodge ball or roller-skating. Hull's Brewery was right up the street, and sometimes when the trucks were out on delivery, the kids would all go home and get brooms, then do a group sweep of the brewery yard, cleaning out the bits of glass and other debris, making the black tar parking lot into one gigantic unbroken field of smoothness. Their steel skates, clamped onto the soles of their shoes, delivered a sweet gliding ride impossible to achieve on cement sidewalks. Here they needn't concern themselves with bumping into people, or turning around when they came to the end of a block. Some of the kids had only one skate, so they would trade back and forth to make a pair and then take turns.

A few of the boys had bikes, most of them rather broken down, but they were good at putting together different parts to create whole bicycles. Ralphie was a genius at it. And sometimes a few of the kids could even afford the 25 cents an hour that it cost to rent a bike. Everyone wanted to ride the rented ones.

Those who were on foot stood around in groups, talking, or playing dodge ball, or jump rope until it was their turn to ride, when they would trade places, leaving the dismounted rider to turn the rope or throw the ball.

Sometimes a group of them would go to Woolworth's or the local drugstore and swipe some goodies, then go to Francine's, whose mother was hardly ever home, or to Aleta and Ralphie's, or to Puddin's. These were the homes where the parents were most relaxed about the kids hanging out. Each of these homes also had a record player, so they'd sit around listening to music and they'd munch, tell jokes, talk about all kinds of things, and dance. Nobody cared who danced with who—girls with girls, boys with girls, or even with other boys. They showed each other the latest steps and laughed at their own awkwardness.

During the spring of the year Aleta turned 13, things started changing in such tiny little ways that she didn't really notice at first.
Little conversations seemed to happen all around her. The girls were whispering behind their hands, and the boys were murmuring with their heads together. Looks were being exchanged, and certain people were dancing consistently together. Every time Aleta turned around, someone was putting on "Out of the Blue," Hadda Brooks' hit song, her smoky sultry voice crooning:

Should love for-get you
for-get he ever met you.
True love will say howdy to you
out of the blue...

Then if you found him
just put your arms around
him
you'll know where or when or how
it happened to you
out of the blue

Aleta liked the song too, but now the boys were pairing off with girls whenever it was played, and the girls never seemed to be dancing together any more. This particular afternoon, as they sat around Puddin's living room munching popcorn and potato chips, Aleta noticed that three couples were dancing close together. The laughter and joking had disappeared altogether, and there was a strange feeling in the room. Ralphie was dancing with Puddin, who had her arms draped over his shoulders, her head tucked into the side of his neck. Aleta thought back to a couple of Saturdays ago, when Ralphie had asked her if she would go to a party with his friend Sonny. She said, "Well, of course I will. Aren't you going too?"

"Yeah, but I'm going with Puddin," Ralphie said.

"Well, I'm going with Puddin too," Aleta said, looking at him in surprise. "Don't we always go together?"

"Oh, come on, Aleta, will you just grow up?" Ralphie was saying that to her a lot lately.

Now, as she looked at Ralphie and Puddin, and at Francine and Bo, and Ruby and Shorty, Aleta suddenly reached to the floor beside the couch and put down the ball she had been tossing gently from hand to hand. As she stood to saunter over to the door, a couple of them said, "Hey, what's up, Aleta? It's still early, where you going?" She mumbled something about homework, shrugging her arms into her jacket.

Sonny came up beside her. "How about I walk you home?" he said in a soft, funny voice.

"Why do I need you to walk me two blocks up the street?" Aleta asked.

"Let's just say I want to enjoy your company a while longer, "Sonny said, giving her a wide grin.

"Oh, cut it out, will you, Sonny? You can walk with me if you want, but you don't have to *walk me* anywhere. I'm not a dog."

"O.K. then, let's go," he said, chuckling and shaking his head as he muttered under his breath, '*I'm not a dog.*' Girl, you are *soo* funny!"

They walked in silence for a block, Aleta wondering what Sonny wanted. Finally, as they turned the corner to her house, she stopped and said, "So, is anything wrong, Sonny?" He raised his eyes from the tips of his shoes and looked at her, then glanced quickly away and said, "I wouldn't say that, exactly. It's just that I'd like you to go to the movies with me this Friday night."

"The movies?" she laughed. "That's all? The movies? Sure."

"You will?" He slapped his hands together, a bright smile spreading from one side of his broad brown face to the other. "That was easy. See, Ralphie didn't think you'd want to go."

"Why shouldn't I? Don't we always go to the movies on Fridays? Isn't he going, and Puddin and Ruby and all the rest?"

"Well . . . that, I don't know . . . what I mean is . . . they're going, but . . . kind of in couples, like . . . you know . . . a kind of . . . a date, like. You know?"

The smile was still there, but now it reached only halfway across his face. Aleta stood in shock. Then the anger began welling up. Tears burned behind her eyes and, rather than let them fall, she yelled in his face, "Why? Why? Will you just tell me why?"

He blurted, "Because I really like you. You're smart, and pretty, and . . . and . . . well, you're fun. I never know what you're going to say or do, and . . ."

Just as the last word came out of his mouth, Aleta hauled back and punched him on the side of the jaw. She was as surprised as he was, and, as she saw him fall to the ground, she turned and fled up her stairs. When she opened the door into the hallway, she looked back over her shoulder and saw Sonny lying there rubbing his jaw, and looking up at her with an adoring smile. She slammed the door in disgust and stormed inside.

Lilly was in the living room scrunched into her favorite corner of the couch, reading. She glanced up, scrutinized Aleta with a long penetrating stare, and then dropped her eyes back to her book. Lilly never pried, but had plenty to say if you asked her advice. She didn't have her opera music on, so they both sat in silence.

KayKay stuck her head into the living room, looked from one to the other, and then said eagerly to Aleta, "What's the matter?" KayKay had already started her period a few months before. When people asked her what she wanted to be when she grew up, she always said, "I want to get married and have babies."

Aleta wondered how people could know what they wanted to be when there were *soo* many things *to be*. She didn't believe KayKay really knew either. Receiving no response, KayKay asked again, "What's the matter with you? Something happen, Aleta?" Silence.

The warm odors of dinner and the sound of the news on the radio in the kitchen meant that Mama was home early today. The one time, of course, that Aleta would rather she wasn't. She decided to head into the bathroom, where she could sit on the laundry bag in the corner and think about everything.

Aleta pushed past KayKay, who was standing resolutely in the living-room doorway, curiously studying Aleta's face. Passing through the two bedrooms that opened off one another, Aleta made it only as far as the kitchen, which she had to traverse to get to the bathroom. Mama, rinsing something in the sink, turned and glanced at her as Ralphie slammed the front door and came bounding through the bedrooms into the kitchen. Mama was just saying, "What's wro..." when Ralphie shouted, "Wow, Aleta, you really did it? You punched out Sonny? Yow, ha ha, *everybody's* talking about it. You'll never get *anybody* to ask you out now."

Mama turned from the sink, her deep-set eyes moving from Ralphie to Aleta and back. "What, what did you say?" Her West Indian lilt became clipped and very British at times like this. Ralphie was shifting from foot to foot, almost jumping up and down with excitement. KayKay's eager face showed in the doorway, and Aleta could hear Lilly coming through the passageway into the kitchen; her calm, one word low-voice commanded KayKay, "*Move!*" KayKay immediately obeyed.

"Is this true?" Mama demanded. Aleta nodded as she took a couple of steps toward the bathroom. She didn't know whether to feel defiant or ashamed, so she alternated between the two. "Why?" Mama asked quietly.

"All he did was ask her to go to the movies, Mama, that's all he did." said Ralphie.

Mama turned her head and gave Ralphie one look. He subsided. Lilly smiled. KayKay's eyes darted to each in turn.

Mama said to Aleta, "Stand still. I asked you why you did this."

"I don't know."

"Yes you do."

"Well ... why did he have to mess up everything?"

"By asking you to go to the movies he messed up everything?"

"Well, everybody's starting to act all strange. We can't just have fun anymore like we used to."

"What do you mean?"

"Well, like how we would all play games, dodge ball, stickball, skating, do our marching and making up chants and stuff. Go to the movies or the dances all together, in a group. Now people are sitting all boy-girl, and kissing and passing notes and stuff."

Mama's eyes slid briefly to Ralphie, who shifted uncomfortably, but didn't say a word.

Aleta continued, "I don't want to be going off with only one person, especially somebody like Sonny, who can't even see when something's funny unless it gets pointed out to him. I'd rather be with everybody. Ralphie and Puddin are the most fun, and they're always going off together. It's getting to be no fun at all. So when Sonny talked about going to the movies like a date, I couldn't help it, Mama, I just punched him."

Ralphie couldn't contain himself any longer. "To the ground, Mama. Hey, Lilly, she punched him right down to the ground. And Sonny came running back to Puddin's telling everybody, like he's proud of it or something."

KayKay said, "If somebody asked me out on a date, I wouldn't punch him. Sonny's nice. I think he's funny."

Lilly dismissed KayKay with the tiniest wave of her slim, elegant hand, an infinitesimal shrug of her left shoulder and a slight "pshhht" that passed through her lips. She said, "Well, it looks like he's discovered your inner qualities or *something*. Hey, brace up. I'll show you how to dress and do your nails, and you can stop running around the streets like a hoodlum and learn how to act like a lady. Sonny isn't much of a boyfriend, but you can practice on him and when somebody comes along who's worth going out with, at least you won't be a complete dolt."

Mama had turned back to the sink and Aleta could have sworn for a second that she was laughing, but when she turned around, there was no trace of it. In a voice that had lost its anger, Mama said, "You're coming to the age when this happens. You can't stop it. If you don't want to go out with someone, just say 'No, thank you.' But you can't go around punching people who think they're paying you a compliment. You hear?"

Aleta nodded quickly, then turned and walked stiffly into the bathroom and locked the door behind her. She lunged across the narrow space into the corner and flung herself onto the laundry bag, stifling her sobs in a towel she pulled from the top of the pile.

Everything was changing so fast. First these stupid bumps on her chest—hurting, sore, embarrassing, and ruining the fit of what few clothes she had. When Mama had suggested a brassiere, she refused.
But that didn't do any good, because the bumps kept on growing anyway. Then one after another, Aleta's friends were all starting to bleed and teasing her because she hadn't started yet. Well, she was glad she hadn't. She couldn't figure out why anyone would want to be bothered with such a mess. Why did girls have to have it anyway? It wasn't fair. And the boys' voices were getting all hoarse and crackly and they weren't playing games with the girls the way they used to.
They were showing off and looking around to see which girls were noticing them when they played with each other instead of just having a good time, the way they did before.

Now she couldn't even enjoy everybody's company when they went to parties and movies together. Why should she have to be with only one person? And if they had to pair off, why did Aleta have to end up with Sonny while Ralphie got Puddin? Puddin was *her* friend first. Oh, why were people so stupid? The hot tears squeezed out of her swollen eyes and slithered down her cheeks.

Aleta started to her feet so she could peek at herself in the mirror to see how she looked while tears dripped down the end of her nose. She could just hear Lilly's voice in her head saying, 'Oh, don't be so melodramatic, you're not the saddest person in the world, you know.' She wouldn't let herself look, but she could feel the corners of her mouth pulling up into a strange, trembly smile while her body shook with silent sobs.

Much later, when she heard the banging on the bathroom door, she realized she'd heard it several times before. Mama was saying to KayKay, "Leave her alone."

"Well, what am I supposed to do? I have to go."

"Go upstairs to Ruby's and tell them you need to use their bathroom; we have an emergency down here."

"What emergency? *That's not an emergency.*"

"Not to *you*, I know."

"How long is she going to stay in there?"

"However long she needs to. Go ahead, go on upstairs."

When Aleta unlocked the door and glanced at the clock above the kitchen table, it was 10 minutes past 8:00. Lilly, Ralphie and KayKay had all eaten and dispersed. Mama was sitting at the table, drinking a cup of tea.

"Did you wash up?" Mama asked. Aleta nodded.

"Take your plate out of the oven." Then, as Aleta started toward the stove, "Careful now, get the potholder."

Aleta sat down across the table from Mama and began eating. The meatloaf and potatoes were dried out, but she was so hungry she didn't even care. After a couple of minutes, Mama said, "You don't have to have dates with anybody you don't want to, you know."

Aleta nodded, head down. "I know, Mama."

"But you do have to get a brassiere."

"Okay," she whispered.

"We'll go Saturday, all right?"

Her mouth full and her eyes on the plate, Aleta nodded. When she looked up, she saw Mama watching her, a sad smile on her face.

Stanley

Just after Aleta turned six, Stanley went off to the war. He was the first and only person close to Aleta's family who did. Stanley lived around the corner, but he hung out at the Skerritt's just about all the time. He was slow talking and slow to smile, but when he did, it lit up his whole face. His teeth were small for such a large face, so you could see them in wide, wide array when his broad lips parted slowly, and his smile spread across his blue-black, smooth skin.

Aleta loved to see Stanley smile. His eyes would sort of half shut, and he'd put his head down and slightly to one side as if he was too shy to let you see his entire face so open in its pleasure. Stanley was large, tall like her brothers but also broad. His wrists were thick, his hands huge. Aleta's brothers—especially Wesley and Alan, who were about the same age—said Stanley was a fool for going off to war, but he said he wanted the adventure. And besides, he wouldn't be alone because Sonny Mahoney was signing up to go too.

"Sonny Mahoney? Sonny Mahoney?" Wesley yelled. "Stanley, are you serious? Sonny Mahoney is white!"

"Cut it out, will you, Wesley, you know I know that."

"Then why don't you make sense?" Wesley said.

He started asking Stanley if it made sense for anybody who is black to be going off to fight the Japanese, who were colored, like us. But, Stanley just kept saying he didn't know all that stuff about politics, he just wanted to go.

"And I told you before; I don't like you calling me *black*."

"Will you please wake up, Stanley?" Wesley said. "We're *all* black; it's noble to be black. You can be a Neeegroww when you get outside, but in this house you're B-L-A-C-K, get it?"

Then Alan said gently, "Aw, come on, Stan, don't go off and get yourself killed for these white people's wars, okay? Stay here and live till you find some other kind of adventure to go on, will you?" And, bunching his knuckles together, he bounced his fist gently against Stanley's chin.

Stanley just kept looking away and shaking his head, as if he was already gone off to war. Then he rose to his feet in one smooth move and announced over his shoulder as he headed for the door, "I'm not going to get killed. I'll be back. Just tell your mom and everybody good-bye for me. I have to report tomorrow."

Stanley snatched Aleta up and gave her a hard hug, then pitched her over the arm of the couch so she landed right in the corner like always. As Aleta rolled to a sitting position, she saw his broad back heading out the door and into the hallway.

"Stanley, don't go," Aleta shouted, terrified that he would die.

His voice floated back up through the stairwell, "See you when I get home, Aleta. Be a good girl, now."

Stanley and Sonny Mahoney had attended the same Catholic school in their younger years. Sonny's mother Blanche, Mama's friend, died just after Sonny graduated from high school. Stanley's father had been a very strict man, a Cape Verdean who thought Stanley needed the discipline of a Catholic school so he wouldn't get out of hand like Aleta's brothers had. Stanley's mother Elvira, who said she had hated school because the nuns were so mean to the children, didn't agree with her husband, but she didn't have a lot of say in the matter. Mama said that after Stanley's father died of pneumonia when Stanley was 11, Elvira should have taken advantage of the opportunity to get Stanley out of that school. But by then, Elvira said she felt that taking him out would be disrespecting his father's wishes.

Anyway, Stanley and Sonny stayed friends from elementary school all the way through high school, and then went to work in different places, Stanley at a coat factory downtown on Kneeland Street, the same place where Aleta's brother Alan worked. Sonny was a telephone lineman. They still went to Washington Park and threw footballs around on the few Saturdays they were both free from work at the same time. They'd have a beer together in the bar afterwards. Wesley loved baseball but disliked football, which he said was "too brutal," although he would hang around in the park with the guys, then go to the bar with them for the beer, and they'd all sing Irish songs. Wesley taught Aleta the words to all the songs, "When Irish Eyes Are Smiling," "East Side, West Side," "I Dream of Jeanie with the Light Brown Hair," "Harrigan, That's Me," and even more. Whenever the Skerritt's had family talent shows, usually on rainy days, Aleta would sing some of those songs. Wesley always recited "Casey at the Bat."

Aleta once heard Wesley tell Stanley that Sonny Mahoney was all right, but he didn't know anything that was going in the world and didn't care to learn. Stanley's slow smile appeared, and he said, "That's O.K. by me, Sonny says you're a radical."

"Well, there's hope for him yet." Wesley said, laughing. "He recognizes one when he sees one." So Stanley went off with his friend Sonny to join the war.

For a while, everyone wondered what their friend was doing. Lilly, Ralphie, Aleta, and KayKay would lie in bed at night making up stories about how Stanley was fighting in the war. They liked to talk about him killing the Germans instead of the Japanese—everyone knew the Germans deserved it because of the way they were treating the Jews and Black people. Besides, Wesley and Mama hated that Stanley was fighting colored people, so when the little ones made up their stories, they never included the Japanese. Gradually, Aleta, Lilly, Ralphie, and KayKay stopped talking about Stanley and just went about living through the brownouts, the air raid drills, rationing, and never having anything taste sweet enough. Aleta was nine when Stanley came back home. He looked strange, not like Stanley, but like an older relative of himself. He was thinner. His skin, unlike the robust, gleaming blue-black it used to be, was instead grey-brown and ashy. He didn't look directly at Aleta either, the way he used to, and his smile wasn't really a smile, just a pulling back of his lips in a way that never quite reached his eyes. There was no fun in Stanley anymore.

"Do you still see Sonny?" Aleta asked him.

He nodded, gave that peculiar smile and said, "Yeah, sometimes, sure."

"Were you together in the service?"

"Well, for some of the time, anyway, not right away."

"What do you mean?"

"Look, Aleta, Stanley doesn't like to talk about it that much. Just give him a rest, O.K?" Wesley said. Aleta nodded, promising herself never to ask again.

Stanley went back to work in the coat factory, and they didn't see as much of him. About a year later he came around with a girl named Maxine, who was tall and dark, pretty and stylish. He introduced her as his future wife. He seemed happier. They were planning to buy a house because he could get the money for a down payment since he was a veteran.

"Where's the house, Stan?" Mama asked.

"Dorchester, out near Codman Square," he said.

Mama frowned. "Son, you think you're going to get a house out that way? There are nice houses for sale around here in Roxbury. Why not stay in the neighborhood? Why be such a distance from everybody who loves you, especially when you start having children?"

"Oh, Mama, say what you mean," Wesley said. Then, he turned to Stanley, "Listen, man, those white folks are going to give you a rough time, no matter how many of their necks you fought to save. It's one thing going into their bar to have a beer and singing their songs with them after a little ball playing. It's another to be trying to move next door to them. What's the point? Really, the houses around here are nicer anyway. Cheaper too."

"It's my right to live wherever I want," Stanley said quietly.

"No one disputes that, Stanley," Mama said. "You just go right ahead and do what you think is right."

He perked up. "You know, Sonny's the one who told me about the place right across the street from him.

"Psshhht, c'mon, Sonny?" Wesley snickered. "You really think he's aware enough to know how these stupid rednecks act when someone black moves into their neighborhood? I wouldn't be surprised if they lit a cross as a welcoming ceremony for you."

"I'm doing it, Wesley. Sonny and me go back a long ways; he'd let me know if anything was wrong. Besides, I took care of him over there, and he's not going to forget that."

Aleta slipped in before anyone could stop her, "You did, Stanley, you took care of Sonny? How?" Mama, Wesley and Alan directed disgusted looks at Aleta, but Stanley started talking right away. His girlfriend Maxine was leaning forward looking interested too.

"Well, I don't know if you heard, Aleta, but I was captured by the Japanese?"

Aleta shook her head, astonished. When she glanced at Wesley and Mama, she could see that they knew, and a sudden anger blazed in her. Why hadn't they ever said anything?

But Stanley continued, "We were in the Philippines and we had a long march to get to where the prison camp was. When we got in there, I was so exhausted I fell asleep. I don't know how long it was before I woke up, but when I did a Japanese soldier was holding my head and dribbling water into my mouth. My tongue felt so big it was hard for the water to even trickle down my throat. Then they gave us a bowl of rice and told us to eat slowly because it had been so long since we'd eaten. I'd just taken about two spoonfuls when I looked up and they were bringing in a group of about ten white soldiers. They looked terrible, like they'd been starved and beaten. One of them looked like Sonny, but he had so much stubble and was so much thinner than I'd ever seen him that I couldn't be sure. We just kept staring at each other, and I could tell from the way he looked into my eyes before he looked away that it sure was Sonny. We were both careful not to say anything to each other because all we were supposed to say was our name, rank and serial number. To tell the truth, if I had been asked anything about Sonny, I wouldn't have known anything to tell about him because we'd never seen each other at all since we went down to report for duty."

"Oh, I always thought you two were together," Aleta said.

"Well, the army doesn't think black and white soldiers can live and work together," Wesley said, with no expression in his voice.

"But, toward the end they changed those rules, but by then we were already POWs." Stanley said. "So, anyway, they sat the white soldiers across the room from us and gave us food and water and made them watch us eat. The Japanese officers were saying things like, 'See, we treat you better than you get treated at home. They hate you for your brown skin. They don't give you this good treatment. Why are you over here fighting against people who have brown skin like you?' "I couldn't just keep eating and watching Sonny and those guys suffering like that. So I turned my bowl upside down in front of me. The officer in charge came over and handed me another bowl, but I wouldn't take it. He kept on holding it out then he turned to the white soldiers and said, 'I wonder how many of you would refuse to eat if we fed you and let them watch. White men don't have that kind of loyalty to colored men, do you? Aren't they supposed to be your slaves? Aren't they your performing monkeys? Don't you say they have tails?' "Then officer waved his hand, and the Japanese soldiers brought water to the colored soldiers. I said to the other guys, 'The Geneva Convention says they're supposed to give us food and water and keep all of us alive. We're all Americans here, guys.' "I said it fast because I didn't know if he was going to let me get it out of my mouth or shoot me, or what. The officer said to me, real soft," 'Oh, we'll feed you alright, mister loyal colored American soldier.' "And he laughed and jerked his head to his men. Then two of them held my arms behind my back and another one started stuffing rice in my mouth. I was spitting it out as fast as they stuffed it in. Then I heard this sound start popping all over the room, and I realized it was the other colored soldiers turning their bowls upside down, rice and water bowls, and the white guys were cheering us, and some of us were crying and some of us were laughing."

"The Japanese wouldn't feed us or give us anything to drink for the next two days. But when they started feeding us, they fed us all equally. We were kept separated, colored from white, but sometimes after they came around with our food, we could hear the white soldiers through the walls shouting, 'Thanks, you guys over there. We'll never forget this,' and all other kinds of stuff. Now, only Sonny and I knew that I did what I did mainly because of him. We rode back on the ship together, and we talked about it, and he said he'd been wondering if the tables were turned would he have done the same thing. Sonny said he'd like to think so, but he'd never really know."

"How awful that he doesn't know." Maxine said.

"Yeah, that made me feel bad. It haunted me for a long time and really put some distance between us. I didn't know what to make of it. If Sonny had been in the same position, he might have let me die."

"It was honest of him to say so, Stanley," Maxine said, "He didn't say he wouldn't have done it, just that he didn't know."

"Yeah, that's what I finally told myself, just so I could try to forget it. Somebody doesn't know what they can do until they get into the situation. We still talk and everything, but it's not the same. And that could just be that we've seen so much, and we're older too. He's married, you know, and I'm about to be." He smiled into Maxine's eyes and reached for her hand. She linked her fingers in his and smiled back at him.

"Anyway, he sure does owe you, no doubt about that," Wesley said. "So, maybe you'll be alright out there in Codman Square with Sonny, who knows?"

But he wasn't. When it came down to it, Sonny couldn't deliver. Some of the neighbors got really upset when they saw Stanley coming around to visit, and told Sonny in no uncertain terms that he'd better not even think about showing that house to Stanley.

Stanley told Sonny not to worry about it, that together they could turn folks' minds around. He tried to convince Sonny to call a neighborhood meeting and tell people that he felt he owed Stanley his life. Sonny wouldn't do it.

It took longer than a year, but after a while, Stanley and Maxine got married. They moved into an apartment on the first floor of the house Stanley bought, the same house he'd grown up in, where his mother still lived on the second floor. Two years later, they had Stan, their first child, named after his father. Then came a girl, and another boy.

Stanley and Maxine's family became Aleta's learning lab for babysitting. By the time she was fourteen, Aleta had learned from Maxine how to diaper, give baths, have patience in reading the same story 50 times in a row, and how to discipline with kindness. Aleta also gained an enormous respect for Maxine's capacity to keep a secret.

Early one afternoon when Maxine arrived home lugging two shopping bags along with her quota of library books, Aleta had just put the youngest two children in bed for naps and sent six- year-old Stan up the back stairs for his regular visit with his grandmother. Because it was one of those rare moments when Maxine and Aleta could sit together completely alone, Aleta seized the opportunity to ask what it meant that Stanley sometimes cooked rice and took it out of the house. Maxine gave Aleta a long, penetrating stare, moved toward the stove, and in silence began brewing a pot of tea. Aleta sat absolutely still, watching the hands on the clock across the room move forward for 12 full minutes. After pulling a tea cozy over the pot, Maxine kicked off her shoes, brought the pot and two cups and saucers to the table, and proceeded to tell Aleta the whole story. That was another plus in a long list of good things about Maxine. She would either tell you something or not. But if she decided to tell, you didn't have the feeling that she was leaving all kinds of gaps along the way.

"I know you'll never tell anyone about this, Aleta. Stanley told me, he could get into trouble. But even beyond that, it's very personal to him." Maxine didn't wait for Aleta's nod, but rushed into the story, obviously glad to be telling somebody about it.

"Unlike my brothers," she began, "Stanley had never learned to cook. But one day, shortly before the birth of Stan, I came home, and on the stove, I found our largest pot with scorched rice stuck to the bottom, and no rice anywhere in sight. When I asked Stanley if he'd thrown it out, he wouldn't answer."

"Just didn't say anything, anything at all?" Aleta asked. "Or was he just trying to put you off?"

"No, he just said," 'I'm not going to tell you because I don't want to lie to you about something I might get in trouble for.'

"I said, 'Trouble? Over a pot of rice? Stanley, what in the world are you talking about?'" He just hugged me and went on into the bedroom. "You know, Aleta, I wouldn't be telling you this if I didn't know how much you care for Stanley."

"And if I hadn't seen him carry rice out of here a few times and asked you what he was doing," Aleta teased Maxine.

Maxine smiled briefly, then continued, "Well, anyway, after that first discovery, I'd see him cook a pot of rice occasionally, and then he'd put it into a big bowl, then put the bowl in a shopping bag and go on out the door, usually at night. And then about a month ago, it all became clear. He'd taken Stan out with him on a Saturday, and when they got back, he sent Stan inside and told him to let me know that he wouldn't be home until later that night."

'Daddy has to wait for the man to get his car fixed.'

Maxine asked, 'What man, what car?'

'The man that drives Daddy to throw out the rice.'

"Aleta, my heart was beating so fast, knowing I was about to find out if what I had been thinking was true. I asked Stan, 'Where does Daddy have to go to throw out the rice?'

'To that man's house, out there where all those pretty houses are at, Mum. The one where Daddy knows the man.'

'Does he throw the rice, Stan?'

'Naw, he just turns the bowl right upside down on the doorstep, or in the yard or anywhere. Daddy said it doesn't matter where he puts it, any where's alright, just so the people in the house can see it.'"

"So what happened?" Aleta asked Maxine. "Did you ever say anything to him about it?"

"I was still waiting up when he came in. 'So did you finish your job?' I asked him. "He didn't say anything for a few minutes, and I was wondering if he was going to answer."

"Then he said, almost in a whisper," 'What do you mean, my job?'

"You know what I mean, Stanley. Come on, baby, tell me why you do it? Oh, I guess I know why, I just don't know what good it does you.'

'It does me good, Maxine. I *have* to do it.'

'Yes, yes, I know you have to do it, but what does it help inside of you to do it? Please, try to explain. I need to understand.'

'It's just that . . . it makes me feel . . . Oh, I don't know, kind of like he's taken something so precious from me, and if I don't make him remember, it's so easy for him to act like it didn't happen.'

'What do you think he's taken? You're the one who acted bravely —with humanity. You're the one who fulfilled what your religion and your family taught you. You're a man, Stanley. He's not. And don't you think he knows that?'

'Yeah, I've told myself everything you're saying. But he's the one living out there in sunshine and trees and wide grass lawns, isn't he? Look where I'm raising *my* family!'

'We live in a lovely, spacious apartment, Stanley. You bought this house you once lived in as a tenant. You support us well, adore your family, work hard, save your money, and help your mother. You're the man of my dreams.' "I tried to move closer and take him in my arms but he moved away and kept talking."

"Then Stanley said," 'I wasn't looking for a reward for what I did, but I expected Sonny to at least look me in the eye and explain to me why he can't act like a man instead of like some redneck cracker, and at least tell me he's sorry.'

"And I said," 'Stanley, please, baby, please don't torture yourself like this. Just face it, Sonny's a coward. His conscience must be bothering him too, but he's just plain scared, can't you see?'

'Sure, I know that. But I was scared too. I had a lot more to lose than he did, and I didn't hesitate but for a few seconds. He's had years, *years* to do better than he's doing. But I won't let him just go on with business as usual. I could understand it better if he was raised like some red-necked cracker, but he wasn't raised like that. Poor old Blanche must be spinning like a top in her grave, seeing Sonny doing this. I despise him, and I'm not going to let him rest from it for the rest of his life. I want you to understand, Maxine, but I guess you can't.'

'I do, darling, I really do. It's just you I'm concerned with. I don't want you to be still hurting so much about it. You'd be so unburdened if you could just let him go.'

'I wish I could, but I can't. He deserves it.'

'Of course he does, he deserves even more than that, but God will punish him.'

Maxine's eyes returned from their faraway gaze and she looked at Aleta, laughing full out.

"Aleta, when I said that, his eyes jumped with joy. He said, 'You mean that, girl, do you really mean it?'

"I said," 'Of course I do. You know God don't like ugly, He'll get Sonny yet.'

'No, no, I mean the other thing you said, about how he deserves even more than I'm doing to him right now.'

'Yes, Stanley, I mean it. I just don't want *you* to be the one who does it to him, that's all.'

"Aleta, Stanley reached out and grabbed me and hugged me like crazy."

"And he said," 'Ah, you couldn't have said sweeter words, girl. As long as you understand, that's all I ever wanted; just for you to understand. It's going to be better now, I promise you. It's going to be better.'

'Stanley, do you mean you're going to stop dumping rice on Sonny's property?'

'Well, I don't know, really. You see, I only do it when I can't stand thinking about it anymore and I have to do something, just to keep from going and hurting him physically, you understand?'

'Yes, I do.'

'But I just get the feeling that I'm not going to be needing to do it as much as before.'

'Oh, I hope that's true, Stanley, I really do.'

'Yeah. And, I wonder if I ended up halting it altogether, how Sonny would feel then?'

'I expect he'd really have a problem.'

'Yeah, he'd keep wondering when I'd be coming with more rice. Then he'd . . . he'd . . . have to . . . Aw, you know what I mean.'

'Sure. He'd have to cook his *own rice* and dump it for himself.'

Maxine threw back her head and laughed. Aleta laughed along with her.

Then Aleta asked, "Did Stanley think that was funny?"

Maxine nodded. "Yes, we both laughed. And I knew he understood because he said, 'Yeah, let him take care of his own damned conscience.'"

Aleta poured the last of the lukewarm tea into both mugs. They picked them up and touched them carefully together in a soft "thunk," as little Stan came through the kitchen door from the back hall in a rush. At the same moment, Stanley's heavy, steady tread came marching down the hallway. As he poked his head through the doorway, he said, "What are you two looking so happy about?"

Aleta grinned at Maxine, who was giving her a long, slow wink as she brought her cup to her lips.

History Lesson

Aleta entered the classroom early and chose the first seat in the second row so she wouldn't miss a thing. In all her years in school, she never had a black teacher!

When Miss Handy entered the room, she turned deftly and held one crutch under her arm as she closed the door behind her, then made her way to her desk. She sat down and reached out to prop her crutches in the corner. Looking calmly out at her new class, she said in a soft, melodious voice, "Hello, girls."

"Hello, Miss Handy," everyone replied.

Aleta dropped her eyes in embarrassment because she hadn't expected the whole class, high school juniors, to respond in such a singsong manner. When she looked up, Miss Handy was smiling directly at her, out of a heart-shaped face with the most beautiful dark brown eyes Aleta had ever seen. She smiled back, her heart beating hard.

Suddenly Aleta realized that, although she'd seen Miss Handy during her entire sophomore year, she had never heard her speak, and certainly had never before looked her directly in the face. Miss Handy was a smooth cinnamon color, with very black shiny straight hair, which she wore twisted into a figure eight bun, low on her neck. Tiny little threads of white hair, faintly visible, were mixed in with the black, and delicate pink lipstick emphasized her dainty mouth.

For weeks Aleta gazed, lost in Miss Handy's beauty, before she finally began paying attention to what she was saying in class. It took several more weeks before Aleta could reluctantly bring herself to admit that Miss Handy was, at best, a mediocre teacher. As hard as Aleta listened, she could *discern absolutely nothing* between the lines. Miss Handy taught the history book just like any other ordinary teacher. In fact, Miss Green, a white teacher in Aleta's previous school, Girl's Latin, was much more stimulating and informative.

Miss Handy took a strong liking to Aleta. Since this was the last class of the day, she asked Aleta to help carry her pocketbook, schedule book and a few other things out to the taxi that she rode home in every day. Then Miss Handy began giving Aleta a lift as far as the corner of the main avenue, to cut down on the distance Aleta had to walk to get to dance school, something she couldn't do when she was at Girl's Latin.

One day Miss Handy asked if Aleta would come to her house and help her do some cleaning on a day they had off from school because it was President's Day.

Miss Handy lived in the first floor apartment of a house she owned, filled with lots of "good sturdy furniture," as she often said. Her house was about six blocks from the school where she and Aleta had met. The dancing school was six blocks in the opposite direction.

It was awkward at first, being in the teacher's home with her, but they slowly found a rhythm for working together. Aleta cleaned out cabinets as she climbed on stools to change the shelf paper and wash the greasy wall above the stove with Spic and Span; Miss Handy telling her when to get down and change the water.

After the success of their first day together, Miss Handy asked if Aleta could come two days a week and half a day on Saturday, but Saturday was out of the question for Aleta. She had to do her housework at home in the morning so that she could be at dancing school by one o'clock. That's where she stayed till evening, taking classes and helping to teach the little ones.

Aleta would never give that up, not even for a hundred dollars a day. It was a sacrifice to give up any time at all, even on weekdays— because she needed to take as many classes as she could. Aleta started dancing at fourteen, which was almost too late, unless you were willing to work like a demon, which she did. But she needed to make more money because her dance equipment was very expensive—she went through a pair of toe shoes every 4 weeks, and that was *no joke for poor folks*, as Mama said. But, Miss Handy seemed to really need her, so they made a compromise. Aleta would ride home from school with her, On Tuesdays and Fridays, work two hours, and then run to her dance school.

One day Miss Handy said she wanted to get a good head start on her spring cleaning because she had neglected to get it done the previous year, and now that she had Aleta, they would be able to do "a very good job, I'm sure, right Aleta?" "Yes, of course, a very good job, Miss Handy, I'm very sure," Aleta said, with a broad smile. And so they began.

Sometimes they would move the sofas in the living room and clean dust balls out from behind. Aleta would slide under beds and pull things out, opening containers of sweaters and blankets that had been folded away for 30 or 40 years, changing the mothballs, refolding the items, and putting them carefully away again.

Miss Handy had a grand piano, two couches and three armchairs, three bedrooms with under bed containers stuffed with blankets that needed to be aired out and refolded, two kitchen tables, four sets of dishes, numerous cups and saucers, miscellaneous plates, drawers full of silverware that needed polishing, and an endless, crowded supply of things to be cared for, and put away again. Aleta's father, who died before she could remember what he looked like, had insisted on getting a grand piano, even though it was a second-hand one. Aleta never told Miss Handy that her family had a grand piano just like hers.
Somehow, she sensed Miss Handy wouldn't like it.

Sometimes Aleta wanted to accept a sweater or scarf that Miss Handy offered, but she had her own rules about such things that she had worked out over a period of time. Mama or no one else knew on what basis Aleta would say yes to one item and no to another. But she herself knew, even though she wouldn't explain the reason to anyone else.

Some of the white women Mama worked for in Newton and Brookline had girls who had outgrown, or maybe just grown tired of, some clothes that were perfectly good and still in style. Accepting clothes from them was okay because Aleta didn't ever expect to see them anyway, so what difference did it make?

Taking something that her friend Em had tired of was okay too. Aleta and Em had long ago dealt with the reality that Em was financially better off than Aleta. Still, although Aleta envied Em's large, quiet neat house and the huge bedroom Em had all to herself, Em envied Aleta's family, her chaotic and bustling home life, and her freedom. Em was generous from the heart, and loved to see Aleta in something she'd given her, so they were both comfortable with their arrangement.

But somehow it didn't feel right to take something from Miss Handy. Aleta would be embarrassed to wear it to school, and Miss Handy would be waiting to see it on her or wondering why she never wore it. Miss Handy gave up offering after Aleta had refused a few times.

The first few times Miss Handy offered Alta cookies and tea, she had refused, thinking it was too much trouble to put Miss Handy through just for her. Then she noticed that her teacher "took tea" herself and seemed to really want Aleta to join her, so she accepted. They'd sit at one of two kitchen tables, the one that was free of piled up papers, folders, letters and newspapers. While they "took tea," they'd "have a chat" as well. Miss Handy seemed quite interested in Aleta's family, and came to know a lot about them over a period of months.

Aleta asked questions about Miss Handy's family, too. Miss Handy said her father had been a dentist. Both parents had lived in the house with her until they died, her mother nine years previously, and the father just two years ago. Miss Handy asked Aleta what she wanted to be when she grew up, and cautioned her to get an education so she'd have "something to fall back on" if dancing didn't work out. Aleta loved her for not saying that an intelligent girl like her shouldn't waste herself on dancing.

"It must be lovely to be able to sail through the air like that," Miss Handy said, smiling into Aleta's eyes. "Can you tell me how it feels?" Aleta felt awkward trying to put it into words, but she did her best to describe the feeling.

"It's like being outside of my body. Just feeling free. The higher and wider you jump, the longer you can float, and if you can time it so that you're up there right at the peak of the music, it's like heaven."

"Do you believe in heaven, Aleta?"

"I guess I don't— not really."

"Have you thought about it?"

"Yes. Have you?"

Miss Handy looked down for a few seconds, then, lifting her head, said quietly, "There's got to be one. There just *has to be*."

"My mother believes in one, but my brother Wesley says you better get it here because this is all there is."

"And you?"

"Well, I just recently read Bertrand Russell's *Why I Am Not a Christian*, and I think I agree with him."

"Bertrand Russell?"

"The British philosopher, Miss Handy, you know him?"

"Well, my dear, who introduces you to such material? Your brother?"

"No. Actually, I was just looking around in the library, and the title caught my eye."

"What does your mother say to that?"

"I don't think I ever mentioned it to her. Why do you ask?"

"Well, if she believes in heaven, she must be a Christian. Would she mind your reading that?"

"Oh no, Mama says the more you read, the more you learn, and if you learn enough, then you can find out what you think."

"Do all of you read indiscriminately like that?"

Aleta laughed. "I think I'm pretty discriminating about my reading, actually. We all are. For instance, Lilly reads tons of *True Confessions*, Ralphie reads nothing but comic books, and Wesley reads all kinds of newspapers and magazines and things like that. We just all read whatever we like."

"And what does your mother think about the *True Confessions* that Lilly reads?"

"Nothing much, but we all tease her about them."

"Is she embarrassed?"

"Only at certain times, like when Wesley says, 'Oh, look, Lilly's getting to the good parts now, her toes are starting to twitch."

They both laughed out loud. "And you, do you read them too?" asked Miss Handy.

"I used to, but there's just so much more interesting stuff to read, I don't bother too much with them anymore."

"What else do you read?"

"I must have read every *Wonder Woman* comic book there is. I still love them. Let's see . . . I read about Pearl Primus and Katherine Dunham, women pioneers in black dance. And . . . oh, yeah, I recently read *The Natural Superiority of Women* by Ashley Montague."

Miss Handy shook her head. "I've never heard of that either."

"Miss Handy, what do you read?"

"Oh, I don't have much time for reading," she said, looking away.

"Well, what's the last book you did have time to read?"

"I read my Bible every night, as I have every night of my life." Aleta watched her silently. "And I'm currently about halfway through *Jane Eyre*. But of course I've read that before; and there's *The Brothers Karamazov*."

"What's that?" Aleta asked.

"A Russian novel, by Dostoevsky."

"Don't you read any American books? Like the kind that tells you what people think about things?"

"Novels tell you what people think about things. They just do it more indirectly," said Miss Handy.

"Then what novels would tell me what people think about things that are American? What novels do you read about black Americans?"

"Aleta, I've been meaning to tell you that there's a certain class of person who doesn't think calling ourselves black will help us much in life."

"Oh, well that's the word we always use in our house. My mother and my brother say all colored people should call themselves black."

"And, there are many colored people who strongly disagree," said Miss Handy in a tone that let Aleta know exactly where she stood. They never did get back to their discussion about reading. In fact, several of their conversations ended up the same way.

One Friday evening, Aleta told Miss Handy she wasn't going to dancing school because she was going to a hall to hear speeches from several people, including Paul Robeson.

"Will he be singing?" asked Miss Handy.

"I don't know about that, but Wesley said he's definitely going to be talking about how the government took his passport away so he can't travel out of the country. And the whole rally is about politics, so he'll be talking about how we as black people have to act to get our freedom."

"Hmmph! He'd do well to raise that beautiful voice of his in song and stop talking so much about all this other business," Miss Handy said.

"You don't like Paul Robeson?"

"Of course I like him," Miss Handy exploded. "It's just that if he persists in all this talk against the government, it will only bring more trouble onto the heads of all decent, God-fearing Negroes. We have enough to go through as it is."

"Well, isn't that what he's trying to do? Get us all to pull together to stop us having to go through so much *as it is?*"

"Aleta, you don't understand. It's just too complicated to solve with all these rallies and meetings. You have to work hard, you have to show what you're worth, and earn respect, and then demonstrating won't be necessary. Nobody's going to give you respect without education."

"Wesley says Paul Robeson has a law degree, and he was some kind of special scholar."

"A Rhodes scholar, yes, that's true. He's received a top-notch education, and he ought to be encouraging others to do the same. Because, you see, the vast majority of us aren't educated yet. That's why young people like you are so important to our future. You must work hard and uplift the race, not tear it down."

Funny, Aleta thought, she was always hearing that expression used in such different ways. She remembered once when she was about eight, when Wesley and Alan had used the same words to Ralphie, who must have been about ten. Her older brothers, who were still living with the family then, were members of a group called The Young Progressives, and they held very secretive meetings at the house, in their bedroom. They had enlisted Aleta and her brother Ralphie and some of their friends to help pass out leaflets about the Scottsboro Boys' trial.

Ralphie said he couldn't pass out the leaflets on Sunday because he had to work at the bowling alley. Wesley and Alan said not to worry about the bowling alley that this distribution was the most important work he could be doing because this was something that was going to *uplift the race, not tear it down* by doing white people's menial labor for them. Besides, they said, being a pin boy was dangerous work, and young boys were constantly having their brains knocked out with bowling balls and flying pins. Ralphie said he was very quick, and hadn't been beaned since the first week he was on the job. He needed some money, he said, and went on out to the bowling alley. The brothers were furious with him, but Aleta was glad that Ralphie was working because he gave her money sometimes. One day, while Aleta and Connie were passing out the leaflets, Connie's older sister, who was Alan and Wesley's age, came along and told Connie to go on home. She said that if Connie kept hanging around with Aleta, she could end up in jail for being a *Communist*. Connie asked Aleta if she was a Communist and Aleta said, "No." She said she didn't even know what a Communist was, so how could she *be* one? Connie stayed with Aleta and they kept right on passing out the leaflets.

That was half a lifetime ago for Aleta, and she wondered how she would ever know whether what she did would *uplift the race*. Would being the best black ballerina uplift the race? What about if she was only 5th best, or 10th? Did people make the decision about what to do with their lives based on whether it would uplift the race? Did Paul Robeson? Did Miss Handy? Could Aleta ask her? Would she ever dare?

One day in early spring, Miss Handy and Aleta had just finished putting away her winter clothes and taking out her summer dresses. They sat down with a cup of tea and Miss Handy told Aleta that she could be in the cotillion if she wanted to.

"The cotillion, what's that?" Miss Handy explained that it was a "coming out" into society for the "better class" of Negro girls. Then Aleta recalled some talk about it at home. Her big brothers had been chuckling about black folks who acted as if the bloodlines to their white ancestors made them better than others with obvious lines direct to Africa; they'd laughed aloud at the notion of a "black society set" built on such ridiculous connections.

So when Miss Handy asked Aleta now about doing this social coming out party, she couldn't imagine that *even if she wanted to* she'd receive any encouragement at home for being part of such a thing as a cotillion. Yet Aleta figured that explaining all this to Miss Handy would be pointless. So she said in as plain a voice as she could, "No, thank you." But, Miss Handy continued. She told Aleta that she had as much right to be in it as anyone else. Aleta nodded to be polite but didn't answer.

A few days later, Miss Handy brought it up again. "You're just as smart and just as pretty as all the other girls who will be entering. I'd be willing to buy your gown. I know your mother doesn't have extra money for this sort of thing." Aleta shifted on the chair but didn't answer. "This is as important an investment for your future as going to college will be."

"You really think so?" Aleta asked.

"I know it, yes."

"Why?"

"First of all, Aleta, you must realize that Jocelyn, Thelma and all those other bright girls who sit back there in that corner are no better than you." Aleta wondered if she meant bright-*minded,* or bright-*colored.*

"They've just had more advantages in life, but not one of them is a bit smarter."

Aleta wondered if Miss Handy could possibly think she was envying those girls' brainpower, but she thought she'd keep that remark to herself and wait to hear what else her teacher had to say. She had already decided that Miss Handy didn't have anything to share with her as far as history was concerned or literature either. But since Miss Handy had such an interest in the cotillion, Aleta might learn something about her philosophy on society. It might give her an idea about what value all this could have. Mama said, Aleta should always be sure to listen to ways of thinking that were different from her own and her family's; she needed other things to chew on. *No, to ruminate on,* — this was a chance to use her newest word.

Miss Handy continued, "Don't *ever* think low of yourself just because you don't have the right clothes or live in the lovely homes like they do. You study hard and meet the right people, and learn how to dress and carry yourself—and you can have all the advantages they have."

"Miss Handy, I don't think low of myself," she couldn't resist saying.

"Well, just don't let them look down on you because their fathers are doctors and teachers."

"I didn't know anything about their fathers till just now. I don't care about their fathers. Or them either, really."

"Aleta, you have to notice who the important people are in the world if you're going to get anywhere."

"Who's important? Jocelyn and Thelma and them?" Aleta laughed. "They can't even hold a sensible conversation, why would I care what they think? I'm fine with all of them, we get along all right, I just don't pay much attention to them, except . . . well, I wouldn't mind having their clothes. They really do wear some pretty nice clothes. But they're just boring, you know? So why would I want to go to a dance and be with them all evening?"

"It's not them, especially, Aleta, it's being introduced to a higher form of society, traveling in the right circles so you can meet the kind of young men you would want to make your life with."

Aleta laughed. "A higher form of society? Well, thank you, Miss Handy, I know you're trying to help me, but I'll take my chances about finding the *right circles* to travel in."

"You don't understand, Aleta. I know I'm probably not presenting it in a way to help you realize it, but this is a golden opportunity you shouldn't dismiss so quickly. They don't let just anybody come-out at a cotillion, but I know I can help you if you'll just take my word on this."

"Honestly Miss Handy, I'd rather be around other kinds of people who are doing exciting and interesting things."

"But, Aleta, dear, dear child, there's so much trouble you can get into for the rest of your life if you're not careful to associate with the right people. You need to get started in the right direction *now.*"

"I'll find them, the right people for me, out there somewhere. I just have to finish school and get away from here to start my life, that's all."

"Listen to me, Aleta"

"Please stop, Miss Handy, I appreciate your concern but I'm just not interested," Aleta interrupted. The teacher looked at her with a sorrow the girl couldn't fathom. How could it possibly make such a difference to Miss Handy? Why wouldn't Miss Handy just leave her alone? Then Aleta thought to ask, "Have you ever gone yourself, Miss Handy? To a cotillion, I mean?"

Her eyes flashed. For the first time Aleta saw a bitter twist to the dainty pink lips. "Well, yes," she said mockingly. "My father took me, all dressed up in my beautiful blue gown that came down to the floor." She looked down at her wasted legs. Her voice grew soft, "And one by one the children of my father's friends came by our table and sat dutifully for a few minutes before they waltzed off." She raised her eyes full of pain to Aleta. "I wish I could have been like you, not wanting any of it. How did you get like this, anyway?"

"I don't know—my family, I guess," Aleta said without thinking. Then, suddenly seeking more clarity, she added, "Like what? How'd I get like *what*?"

"Arrogant," Miss Handy spat out, her face twisted in anger. "Just so sure of yourself and arrogant! Who do you think you are to be so superior? You have *nothing*, and you think . . . you think . . ." She sputtered to a stop.

They stared at one another for a few seconds before looking away as if by mutual assent. Aleta felt as if she had done something to be ashamed of, maybe by asking too many questions. Miss Handy looked as if she herself *knew* she had.

After a few minutes of silence, Aleta gathered her things and left, closing the door softly behind her. Neither of them said goodnight.

Aleta went back only twice more; it just seemed best to make an excuse about extra rehearsals. Miss Handy made no objection; in fact, she seemed relieved. But whatever she was feeling toward Aleta, she gave her an A- in American History. Aleta had never received less than an A in her life, but Miss Handy just couldn't give her a perfect grade. She needed to do that for *herself*, Aleta thought. If that's what made Miss Handy feel better, so be it. Aleta was free.

Cambridge view of Boston 1980s

JJ and the VV

Head lowered, hands shoved deep into her pockets, Aleta trudged along the cold, grey, early October beach at Plum Island, where the dull damp sand held firm the footsteps of some previous walker. Off in the distance, Jessica sat reading on the blanket; a foam cushion laid carefully underneath to buffer the chill of the ground. They were the only two people as far as Aleta could see in both directions along the entire beach.

Aleta couldn't even remember what they thought they were doing here. Oh, yes—she felt the corner of her mouth quirk—they had come to get away from the problems of home, just the two of them, to reconnect. If Jessica hadn't already made the off-season reservations and paid for the room with their pitiful little resources, Aleta would have called the whole thing off. It seemed as if they did nothing but argue these days. And although the spats over the kids, the apartment, the car and all manner of other things seemed possible to overcome, the ever escalating battle around their differences over the Palestinian issue looked as if it would rend their relationship past repair.

The discussions had commenced a few months after their friendship began four years previously, but in those delicate days of new beginnings, whenever they'd touched on it, they'd shied away, neither of them wanting to probe too deeply the tensions they knew were lurking there. Gradually, as they grew more comfortable with one another and more certain of their own positions, they had begun pointing out articles that supported their own viewpoints, each certain that with logic and time, she could persuade the other. Since the major media was so slanted toward Israel, Aleta felt that she had a harder time discovering unbiased articles to share with Jessica.

After a while, Aleta realized that giving them to Jessica made her resentful, so she stopped. Lately, they discussed the Palestinian issue only if it got thrown in their faces. And, as the Palestinians became more adept at throwing it in the face of the world, incidents that called for discussion came more readily into their lives. After each one of their discussions, Aleta would vow not to talk to Jessica about Palestine ever again. But, she knew that was an empty promise. Their relationship had been conceived in a shared view of politics. Neither of them could be with a lover who didn't share the same values at their very core.

Last night after the news, Aleta had clicked off the TV and headed into the kitchen and straight to the sink, determined not to say a word about the report they had just seen.

Jessica followed, dropping into a chair at the table and announcing in a careful voice, "I thought that was a fair report."

Aleta silently poured a trickle of dishwashing liquid, turning the water on in a hard rush. Friday was twelve-year-old Zarina's turn to wash the dishes, but she was staying at her grandmother's tonight because of Aleta and Jessica's trip tomorrow. Jessica persisted, "That was okay, wasn't it?"

Aleta glanced back over her shoulder, throwing her words abruptly, "Of course you'd be satisfied. How many times did he use the word terrorist when talking about Palestinians? Five? But still not enough for you, I'll bet."

"Oh, come on, he only said it a couple of times. Besides, what else can you call people who blow up innocent women and children?"

"Depends." Aleta turned around and leaned against the sink, arms swiftly folded across her chest. "I might call them people at war, I might call them guerrillas, I might call them killers, I might call them short-sighted, I might call them desperate, I might call them Palestinians, I might call them Israelis, I might call them Jews. But you'd call Israelis or Jews *anything* but terrorists, and that's why I think we'd better call this whole conversation off. You can't be fair."

Her voice was shaking. Kwame's bedroom door opened and he stomped upstairs to the bathroom, shutting the door behind him with a click decidedly louder than his usual quiet closing of doors and light movement through their crowded duplex apartment. The clear announcement of displeasure from the sixteen-year-old brought no pause in their escalating argument.

"Fair? Fair?" Jessica's voice climbed an octave. "You think that murdering dog Arafat is fair?"

"I'm not going to stand here and listen to you call the man a dog. I've never called Begin, Sharon and all the rest of them who slaughtered Palestinians dogs, have I?"

"Slaughtered!" Jessica yelled. "You'd better think about yourself and what you claim to be your non-racist beliefs. You're showing your own anti-Semitism."

"Oh, please, you ought to be ashamed to lie like that to justify your own blindness."

"You ought to be ashamed yourself. Your whole family is anti-Semitic, you admitted it to me."

"What? What's my family doing in this?" Aleta screamed.

Kwame pounded down the stairs and re-entered his bedroom, slamming the door.

"I know it doesn't suit your purpose to remember this, but I once told you that my mother said if my father had lived, we would all be Jewish because he wasn't pleased with Christianity. And I told you that growing up, poor though we were, we had three little containers for donations on our mantelpiece: one for church, one for the NAACP, and one for Trees for Israel. Does that sound to you like an anti-Semitic family?"

"Yes, I remember. I also remember that you said you were glad you weren't Jewish."

"Of course. I also said I was glad I wasn't Christian, either, no matter what denomination. I was simply glad I had seen through it all and refused to be part of any organized religion. Because I refused to be organized into a group where I'm part of some flock with the beliefs and rules all set that I can't participate in altering. You agreed with me then. Or *pretended to*, anyway. But, I suppose that statement now makes me anti-Semitic. You're too much for me, girl. I just can't keep up with all your twists and turns."

"Well, your sister Julie's anti-Semitic, and you know it. She showed it the first night we met."

Aleta threw up her hands. "Is that supposed to be something new? We've talked about that before, several times. She baited you in a snide way about eating pork. I'm not defending her on that crap. Still, that's a far cry from your mother calling me a Schvartze, you know. But do you hear me condemning you and your sister for what your mother says? Anyway, you said my whole family is anti-Semitic, and Julie is not my whole family. Furthermore, she's not the person in my family I share politics with."

"You share politics with your precious brother Wesley, and you told me what he said yourself."

"I know exactly what you're referring to, and as usual, you've twisted what I said to suit your own lame argument. I told you that when I was in grade school and so elated over Israel's becoming a nation, Wesley warned me that this day would come. He said there were people living there first, and that our chickens would come home to roost. That's anti-Semitic?"

"Our chickens would come home to roost? The same damn words Malcolm X used when Kennedy was assassinated? And, by the way, he was anti-Semitic too."

"And there's more to that story than what you heard. The phrase has been around for many a year, you know; he didn't coin it. And by the way, for someone who mistrusts whatever the media says about women, you're remarkably gullible about whatever they feed you about Palestinians, black or brown people or any other people of color. And don't bother to start again about Imiri Baraka, or Farrakhan either. I'm the one who first talked to you about those guys and told you what I think of them—and I refuse to be put into a bag with them. If you start that again, you have to admit you're the racist. They've got nothing to do with me. I'm me, you hear? This is between *you and me!*"

Aleta's voice rose as she picked up her pace to drown out Jessica's attempts to interrupt. "Anyway, see if you can absorb this, will you? When I kept insisting to Wesley that my teachers and other people said the land in Palestine was unoccupied, he threw up his hands at the ignorance of the general population and despaired that I would ever become politically aware. He also cried when Patrice Lumumba was murdered in Africa, and then cried more when he realized I didn't even know who Lumumba was. "I know you don't care to hear about Africa right now, but I'm saying what I please, you hear me? Wesley talked to me for a day and a half about the United States' role in the assassination simply because Lumumba was a socialist, the significance of it, and how it was going to affect the emerging nations of Africa. Wesley was a lefty totally caught up in world politics, not an anti-Semite."

"Jessica, my family has been friends with Jews my whole life, long before I ever met you, mostly Jews who were secular, which you *claimed to be* once upon a time. But you select out what you want and put your own weird twist on everything, and I'm goddamn sick of it. Now, if the only thing you can gather from what I told you about Wesley's thoughts on Israel is that he's an anti-Semite, you and I are in worse trouble than I thought."

Jessica rose to her feet, the chair crashing to the floor behind her. "We're in trouble, all right, because you don't care about anyone except the Palestinians. All right, they're brown; all right, they're people of color; all right, you feel solidarity with them. But you don't give a shit about what they do to the Israelis."

"You idiot, the Israelis have the power, what can the Palestinians do to them? If Arafat had any power, he wouldn't have to be traveling around the world, hiding in a different place every night to avoid being assassinated."

"But the Palestinians have the numbers. What do you expect Jews to do? Do you even bother to think about the Holocaust? We have nowhere else to go. You're the one who's blind and bigoted."

"Because I think someone besides Jews have the right to a homeland? And it is Palestinians' land, isn't it? Weren't they pushed out?"

"It belongs to the Jews!" Jessica's face was pushed up into Aleta's, her eyes squeezed shut.

Aleta backed away, yelling, "How do you figure that? Weren't Palestinians living on it when they arrived?"

"It's the ancient, Jewish homeland, *The Promised Land.*"

Aleta laughed derisively. "Why, you hypocrite. I don't believe you just said that, Miss Anti-religionist, you just gave yourself away."

"You ignorant asshole, it's not about religion, it's about my people, a tribe."

Aleta took a deep breath. "Let's stop, O.K.? Please, let's just *stop.*"

"I don't want to stop! I'm not through!"

"Well, I am." Aleta reached under the dishes to let out the water, dried her hands on the towel hanging by the sink, and fled upstairs to bed. Jessica entered the darkened bedroom a few minutes later, still breathing hard, but she didn't speak, she just grabbed her pillow and left. Aleta could hear her pounding down the stairs to the living room, where she would sleep huddled under the afghan on the couch. In the morning they spoke in neutral tones to one another, eyes purposely not meeting as they packed up for their night away.

Aleta was pushed far into the corner of the passenger seat, eyes shut, body curled into a ball, arms folded against her chest, back wedged into the place where the seat meets the door. Jessica drove the little Toyota competently along, the car radio tuned to National Public Radio, just as it was every Saturday morning while they lingered over breakfast at the kitchen table reading the *Boston Globe*. Another incident between the Palestinians and Israelis was being reported on the car radio. Aleta's stomach knotted in tense anticipation. She ignored her impulse to turn off the radio. She didn't want to unfold her arms, nor did she want to interact with Jessica by making even the smallest move. Suddenly, the radio clicked off. Except for the tires humming along the road and the slight sound of wind whistling past the windows, there was silence.

"Thanks," Aleta muttered.

"Aleta."

"Hmmm?"

"You sleeping?"

"No."

"Listen, let's try to have a good time today, O.K.?"

"O.K."

"Would you open your eyes?"

Aleta lifted her head and opened her eyes. Jessica was watching her with a tentative, sad smile.

Then, turning to look at the road, Jessica said, "Let's try not to fight. Let's read and play and eat and make love just like we planned, O.K.?"

Aleta nodded briefly. Jessica continued, "I know you can't stand to touch when you're angry, but maybe if we do the rest of the stuff without arguing, you'll stop being angry long enough to remember that we need to do that too."

"Jessica, it's not about being angry, it's just wondering if . . ."

"Shhh," Jessica lifted her right hand off the wheel and touched her forefinger lightly to her own lips, then reached over and brushed the finger across Aleta's mouth. "Come on, give the day a chance, O.K.?" Aleta felt her gaze but remained silent.

They stopped at a little variety store and Aleta went in to pick up a few items. She spied the *Village Voice* and remembered that she'd meant to bring along the copy from home. Yesterday afternoon, she had stood in the neighborhood Store 24 looking down at the cover of the weekly paper, and had seen the June Jordan poem. She'd read it standing there in the store, then taken it home and read it several more times. Each time she finished, tears welled up in her eyes and she wondered if anyone could read this and still not understand the Palestinian situation.

Aleta couldn't help wishing Jessica would read it. But every time she tried to show her something that presented the Palestinian side in human terms, they'd end up in an argument, with Jessica accusing Aleta of trying to brainwash her. Unable to deny that the accusation was somewhat true, Aleta would become defensive and angry. So, after the awfulness last night, Aleta had been too discouraged to pick up the paper as they were leaving the house this morning, although for one fleeting moment she had thought about it. Now, feeling rather foolish, as well as wasteful for spending $1.75 on a newspaper they already had at home, Aleta snatched it up and tossed it on the counter along with juice, crackers, fruit and gum, and marched back out to the car carrying the bag.

"Did you have enough money?" Jessica asked

"Uh-huh."

"Been thinking about what I said?"

"Yeah. There's one thing I want you to do, though."

Jessica's voice was relieved. "Sure, what?"

"I bought the *Village Voice*."

"Oh, good, what's in it?"

"A poem by June Jordan that I want you to read. It's on the cover."

"June Jordan? On the cover of the *Voice*? Well, allriiiight. Have you read it?"

"Yes,"

"Bet it's great, huh? What's it about?"

"You'll see. Promise you'll read it before anything else?"

"Of course, are you kidding? No problem."

They sang songs the rest of the way — Secret Love, The Impossible Dream, Bye, Bye Love. Jessica had the voice, Aleta the words. Now, making her slow way toward the blanket where Jessica sat with the newspaper, Aleta wondered if Jessica would attack her for the deceit of not letting her know what she was in for with the poem; whether she would retreat from it into angry silence; or use her convoluted analysis to dismiss June Jordan as yet another brown-skinned anti-Semite.

More to the point, Aleta wondered if Jessica had any notion that their relationship was so close to going under. She'd been pushing down the knowledge that had been rising closer to the surface for nearly a year, and she suspected Jessica might be doing the same. The thought of parting was too wrenching; but the reality of continuing to live together across such a chasm was impossible.

This walk had helped Aleta locate the truth she'd been seeking: that if Jessica couldn't look deep into her own heart and fight her way past all the protective barriers set up by a people for survival; if she couldn't get to the basic fact that she was seeing Palestinians as a lesser people than Jews; if she couldn't then make the connection that Aleta as a black woman wouldn't be able to trust her as a white woman carrying such an attitude, then there was nowhere they could go from here.

If the brown Palestinians were dogs, terrorists, animals, murderers and all manner of unspeakable beings because they wanted what any other people wanted, what did that make this black woman Jessica considered herself so in love with? Much as Jessica wanted to put it down to political differences on *this one issue*, as she was fond of saying, Aleta would have to find a way to make Jessica see that it went far deeper, to a fundamental place, to the denial of the Palestinians' basic humanity.

It frightened Aleta to be living and raising her children with anyone who couldn't see that. Out of the chaos of her feelings, she had finally wrestled to the surface what the real battle was about: that this one issue was key to everything their lives rested on, and to whatever they would build together in the future. Is everyone equally human?

That's it. That's just what this is. Her knees shook with relief at finally getting it all sorted out—and with the fear of launching the discussion that she couldn't avoid now that she had the crux of the problem within her sights. She hoped she'd be able to explain it in a way that could allow them to maintain their support for one another as friends, lovers, and life partners.

Aleta had to convey to Jessica that she needed someone she'd never have to question on the basics, or she'd rather have no lover. At least that would leave the possibility that if someone came along who could get to the core of who she was, she'd be free for a relationship. If no one came along, then she'd still be free—and intact.

Aleta knew what Jessica would say: That they'd each survived the devastation of extrication from long-term partners ——Aleta from a marriage of nearly two decades, Jessica from a lesbian decade-long relationship. Aleta had also disentangled herself from a two-year destructive lesbian love affair with a woman who, although she had aggressively initiated the relationship, could never use the word lesbian in connection to herself, and flinched when Aleta used it to describe herself. Jessica had ended an affair with a heterosexual woman who had simply wanted an "experience" with a *dyke*. They'd survived a long-distance romance as Jessica moved to two different cities in three years, until Aleta could finally join her. They had learned how to penny pinch their way through unemployment for both of them at the same time, coped with the anger of hostile adolescents, uprooted from their comfortable home and the only environment they'd ever known.

They'd submerged their hurt from homophobic relatives and slowly persuaded the children to accept their relationship.

After all that, Jessica would say, they could survive this too.

But *this* wasn't something to be survived, overcome, compromised about, worked on. Ultimately, you either got it—or you didn't. There were two sides to the story, with enough bad decisions by both groups to bring them to tears. How could Aleta continue a life with someone who refused to even examine the reason why many people, Jews included, weren't simply demonizing the Palestinians outright without ever considering their plight? Three years of bickering on this one issue was enough. They'd have to face their waterloo. Aleta was hoping they could at least remain friends. Would she be able to overlook this one deep disagreement and still interact with her? Or on some deep level was she just plain racist and unable to examine it?

As Aleta approached the blanket, she could see Jessica lying on her side, watching her. She appeared composed. Aleta looked closer. Jessica was leaning up on one arm; her dark eyes deep and liquidy, tracks of tears sitting calmly on her face.

"I *got* it," she said, smiling broadly.

Aleta stood a few feet away, staring. "Have you been crying?" "Yes, I have. But it's O.K. Because I *got* it. Oh, god, she's wonderful. June Jordan is wonderful!" She threw her head back, face exposed to the cool air, eyes closed.

"It's true, everything you've been saying is true, but somehow she got it into a poem, and I *got* it. You don't believe me, I know, but I really *do* understand."

"Jessica, what . . . I can't believe . . . what are you saying?"

"I'm saying that it's all here. So beautifully and passionately here, you just have to feel it. I couldn't keep on denying their humanity once I read this."

Aleta's trembling knees gave out. She sank slowly onto the blanket, her back to the water so she could look directly into Jessica's face and said, "Read some of it to me."

They said they were victims.
They said you were Arabs.
They called your apartments and gardens guerrilla strongholds.

They called the screaming devastation that they created the rubble.
Then they told you to leave, didn't they?
Didn't you read the leaflets that they dropped from their hotshot fighter jets?
They told you to go.
One hundred and thirty-five thousand Palestinians in Beirut and why didn't
you take the hint?
Go! There was the Mediterranean: You
could walk into the water and stay there.
What was the problem?
I didn't know and nobody told me
and what could I do or say, anyway?

When she finished, they were both in tears. After a long silence, Jessica said, "Oh, if only I could show this to my mother and make her read it."

"Never mind your mother, woman. Consider that you just got it yourself, and look at the progressive politics you've been involved in for all these years."

They talked the entire afternoon in that excited way they used to when they first began exploring each other's minds and ideas. As they took warm showers, sitting in turn on the closed lid of the toilet waiting for one another, Aleta listened keenly to the words tumbling out of Jessica with a speed and level of understanding that kept surprising them both. The torrent continued into the evening as they trudged arm in arm up the dirt road to the little restaurant for dinner.

Aleta began to feel a slight resentment as she heard words being fed back to her that never came from Jordan's poem but from things *she* had said to Jessica throughout many a bitter argument over the course of the years. As they settled at the table in the restaurant, Aleta opened her mouth to speak, but clamped it shut suddenly as Jessica said excitedly, "I know you've said all this to me before, but it's like there was a wall and none of it could get through; not past all those dimes I sacrificed through my childhood to help plant trees in Israel; not past all those silences in my family about what really happened to our relatives in Europe; or the nightmares I had when I gradually learned the truth about those years. I still have the nightmares sometimes, you know that. Ah, but June Jordan. You must have known I could get it through her poem. Somehow it just entered my heart and crashed into my brain. Oh, I'm so glad it got through, but I can't imagine how frustrating, how painful it must have been for you."

"No, you can't," Aleta said solemnly. Then she laughed, shaking her head, "And to think I almost didn't bother. It really seemed so hopeless."

Jessica leaned across the table and said softly, "Thanks for the one last try."

They grinned happily at one another.

"Excuse me." They came out of their own world long enough to look up. The grey-haired, sturdy woman who served the tiny restaurant as counterwoman, cook, cashier and waitperson was standing over them. "I just want to give you your food before it gets cold," she announced, smiling comfortably at them as she set down their plates.

The talk continued through dinner and accompanied them on their slow, arm in arm walk back to their cozy room. They chattered into the night as they lay stretched out on the bed. At some point, one of them would stop the other's words with a kiss. They slid into one another's arms, hugged tight, and entwined themselves comfortably together.

Then one said, "Thank you June Jordan."

The other said, "Thank you, *Village Voice*."

And somebody whispered, "Shut out the light."

Turning Point 1989*

By Jennifer Abod

The way you build love
means deconstructing
false images
stone by stone
moment by moment

The way you build love
when love is barely understood -
is to fight over what's important.

The stony dry arid land of Israel,
a home that I've never known,
nor will ever know;
was an early war-zone.

In childhood dreams
young olive trees standing tall
their slender branches with tender leaves
stretching into the clear blue peaceful sky.

I was about ten, maybe younger,
every week I placed my dimes carefully into the tiny slots on my
Tree Card.
I was helping to purchase trees for a sanctified grove
honoring our dead who fought for their land.

Your questions yanked deeply at images more firmly rooted than I
knew.
I watched your beautiful brown face and sad solemn eyes
as you extended your graceful dancer's arm to hand me
June Jordan's poem. "The blood soaked images of
Lebanon..."
I felt heavy tears fall on my face.

I wiped my eyes
clearing the view for unexamined loyalties and different
truths.

*Abod's poem was written following the argument fictionalized in JJ
and the VV. Jessica is based on her.

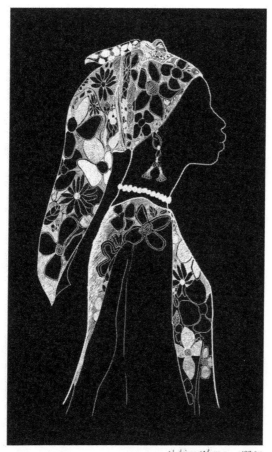

Nubian Woman 1970s

ACKNOWLEDGEMENTS *by Angela Bowen*

"Cornelia's Mother," the first of *Aleta's Stories*, seemed to write itself at The Berkshire Women's Writing Retreat. For over ten years beginning in the early 1980s, I was happily part of a vibrant and diverse feminist movement and culture, which inspired creativity and community.

I have been lucky to cross paths with people who have encouraged my writing and scholarship: Miss Palm, my high school writing teacher, let me know I had talent; Karen Lindsey created a women's writing group in Cambridge; the Barbara Deming Memorial Fund awarded me a writing grant; Clark Taylor encouraged me to finish my Bachelor's degree; Professor Ann Withorn let me know that it was possible to be an activist and a scholar at the same time. I greatly appreciate the women at Clark University for establishing this country's first freestanding Doctoral Program in Women's Studies, and selecting me as one of its first candidates.

This book is possible because the following people donated their work, their talents, skills and passion: Jennifer Abod, my partner of 33 years, pushed me to publish these stories and has been the steady hand at the helm making it happen; Khari Klein worked tirelessly editing and formatting; Becca Wilson copy edited; Virginia Blaisdell designed the lovely book covers; Alan Shwachman gave me permission to use his mother's photos. Ntombi Peters, Honor Hart, Lisa Hartouni and Azaan Kamau generously provided critical technical support whenever they were asked.

Cynthia Rich has supported *Aleta's Stories* for years as has my daughter Ntombi A. Peters, my son Jomo Peters, and my dear friend Marti Smith; Susan Abod has provided wise counsel and sisterly support.

I would also like to thank The Bowen Family, in particular, my mother, Sarah Allen Bowen, who would have loved reading these stories.

PROFILE PRODUCTIONS

Jennifer Abod created Profile Productions in 1988 to produce and distribute media featuring feminist activists and cultural workers, particularly women of color and lesbians who influence broad constituencies.

Award winning audio productions include:

The Edge of Each Other's Battles: The Vision of Audre Lorde
Look Us in the Eye: The Old Women's Project
Calling on Women: A five part radio series
An Audio Profile of Audre Lorde

Currently in Post Production: "The Passionate Pursuits of Angela Bowen," a feature documentary about Bowen's Life.

For more information and how to support Profile Productions projects visit www.jenniferabod.com

Made in the USA
Charleston, SC
23 June 2014